NORTH
KOREA
JOURNAL

NORTH
KOREA
JOURNAL

Michael Palin

HUTCHINSON

INTRODUCTION

FOR MUCH OF THE YEAR I HAD BEEN AWAITING THE go-ahead on what was potentially one of the most demanding, exhausting, but exhilarating acting roles I'd ever been offered. I had taken riding lessons, spent hours on Michel Thomas's Spanish course, grown appropriate facial hair and even had a nose specially made. All so I could take the lead in Terry Gilliam's latest attempt to make the film his life was leading up to, *The Man Who Killed Don Quixote*. But for various reasons shooting had been repeatedly delayed. It was to be July, and then it was to be October, then it was to be neither. As contractual problems confounded any progress, the explanations for my beard and moustache were becoming less and less convincing, as were my reasons for turning down other offers.

Eventually the time came to grasp the nettle, and on an early autumn morning, with sadness and regret, I sat down, composed an email of resignation to Terry, took a deep breath and pressed 'send'.

No sooner had that email gone out, than another came in. It was from one Dan Grabiner at ITN Productions, and was headed, 'I have an unusual one for you today'. I'm used to the unusual but this was very unusual. It was a request for me to consider presenting a series, for ITN and Channel 5, in North Korea.

My philosophy of travel, such as it is, is that the more difficult somewhere is to get to, the greater the prize to be won by getting there. But when the prize was North Korea, I found that this was not a view shared by my wife, and a surprising number of my friends. To many of them, this was a step too far. The known unknowns were one thing, but the unknown unknowns were quite another.

Not that anyone could claim North Korea is a complete unknown. There have been books written about it, and accounts from defectors aired on radio and television. Unfortunately nearly all these accounts speak of a cruel, godless, secretive state whose people live in oppression and poverty under the yoke of a ruthless, self-perpetuating dictatorship. Not an easy sell to the doubters.

At the time ITN Productions contacted me, Kim Jong Un, the current ruler, young and eccentrically tonsured, had been in power for five years, following the death of his father Kim Jong Il who had himself, in 1994, inherited the reins of power from *his* father, Kim Il Sung, the founder of the DPRK – the Democratic People's Republic of Korea.

The North Koreans had few friends in the outside world. The Russians had helped them for a time, but after the collapse of communism in 1991 they backed off, leaving the Chinese to become their reluctant paymaster. Other countries viewed them with increasing suspicion when, despite limited resources, the North Koreans ramped up the stakes by pursuing Songun, a policy which put the military at the heart of the country's existence. This led to the testing of nuclear devices and the building of ever larger intercontinental ballistic missiles. Attempts at reconciliation with the West consistently failed, ensuring that North Korea remained comfortably ensconced on President George W. Bush's axis of evil.

Despite this distinctly unpromising international image, I followed a gut curiosity and replied to ITN that yes, I was interested and I would like to know more.

After a few initial meetings the momentum slackened. The international situation worsened and the idea of a North Korea travelogue looked less and less likely. Added to this, my wife was to have a knee replacement and I needed to be at home to help with her recuperation. I therefore decided to confine myself to another project, and one which would keep me closer to home: following up my new-found enthusiasm for the extraordinary life story of a ship called HMS *Erebus* and turning it into a book.

It seemed to be the right decision. The news from the Democratic People's Republic was going from bad to horrible. Kim Jong Un was threatening the world, boasting that his country had assembled an arsenal of missiles and sixty nuclear weapons to go with them. The immediate reaction of the newly elected American President, Donald J. Trump, was hardly encouraging. Calling the North Korean leader 'a madman', he promised that North Korea 'would be met with fire and fury like the world has never seen'. 'Rocket Man is on a suicide mission,' Trump jeered. Kim Jong Un retaliated, calling Trump 'a mentally deranged dotard'.

The likelihood of my ever being able to film in the Hermit Kingdom was receding by the insult. My wife was relieved, and I reconciled myself to missing out on what would have been my ninety-eighth country.

But ITN and Channel 5 hadn't given up. Throughout the months of belligerent name-calling, they had kept in touch with their chief contact, an English tour operator called Nick Bonner, a man who had been organising tours to the DPRK for twenty-five years and who knew the country intimately.

At the beginning of 2018, Bonner noted more promising signs coming out of North Korea. In his New Year speech, Kim Jong Un, whilst warning that 'the entire US is within range of our nuclear weapons', had extended an unprecedented olive branch to the President of South Korea, and by implication to the world outside. As I grappled with the disappearance of HMS *Erebus* in the Arctic ice, things seemed to be thawing in a very different part of the world.

The DPRK, so long portrayed as the secretive grump of international politics, was embarking on what used to be called a 'charm offensive'. Not only were they sending a team to the Winter Olympics in South Korea, but in a very canny move, they had also decided to dispatch Kim Yo Jong, the photogenic sister of Kim Jong Un, to stand behind the robotic US Vice President Mike Pence at the said Olympics, demonstrating at a stroke that the grumps were in Washington, not Pyongyang.

Almost unbelievably, within a month of the Olympics, the White House announced a possible meeting between the Supreme Leader and the American President. A few weeks later Kim Jong Un left North Korea for the first time since he'd assumed power in 2011, taking a train to Beijing to meet the Chinese President.

Fanned by the warm breeze of rapprochement, expectations were reviving. A production office was set up. Books on North Korea fell through the letter-box. Though I was still working flat out on *Erebus*, I was persuaded to meet up with a potential director, Neil Ferguson – whose own account of the pre-film preparations will be found as a postscript to the Journal. We had to be careful. The project was on such a knife edge that any advance publicity could have killed it off. In a suitably clandestine, John le Carré way we met at tables at the backs of pubs and cafés, and always referred to North Korea as North Croydon.

One stroke of luck was a three-week hole in my *Erebus* production schedule, whilst my editor took a fine-tooth comb to my finished copy. Suddenly, with almost indecent haste, I was packing my bags for the flight to Beijing, assuring my wife that Kim Jong Un was about as dangerous as Father Christmas, and that everything would be fine now that North Korea was looking for friends rather than enemies. In the few quiet moments before departure I knew that I didn't really believe that, and the one thing history told us was that the relationship between North Korea and the rest of the world could change in an instant. This was not going to be like any other journey I'd ever done.

2018

I WAS WARNED THAT BECAUSE THE NORTH KOREANS ARE paranoid about information entering their country, I would not be able to take the basics of all travellers – maps, guidebooks, online advice – into the DPRK. As we were hoping to film right across the country, in cities, towns and countryside, this was an irksome restriction. Along with a corresponding nervousness at being seen to wield a camera or a voice recorder, my options for recording this once-in-a-lifetime journey were confined to a small ring-backed blue notebook, chosen to be as inconspicuous as possible.

In the event, the authorities were pretty tolerant of my iPhone camera and in the privacy of various hotel rooms (though privacy was something we remained sceptical about) I was able to add supplementary material on my voice recorder. Though I've tidied it up a bit and augmented the entries with memories that I never had time to write down, the bulk of this account was scribbled in the blue notebook whenever I had a moment.

One thing I did learn is that North Korea is not a label the locals acknowledge. They know their country as the Democratic People's Republic of Korea – the DPRK.

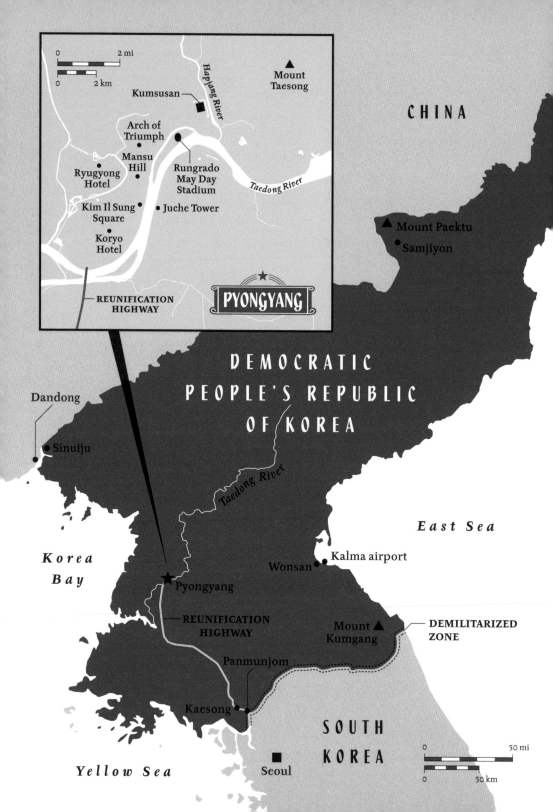

DAY 1

THURSDAY 26TH APRIL

ABOARD B.A. FLIGHT 39 TO BEIJING. WINDOW SEAT.
It's seven in the morning as I push the shutter up after a night of patchy sleep. Craning forward I can see below me the brown, dusty, spectacularly barren Mongolian desert. This must be the Gobi. Everyone else has their shutters closed, but for me the choice of snoozing or the Gobi Desert is a no-brainer. These are the lands where invasions began. It was from this hard-baked maze of mountains that Genghis Khan led his warriors to conquer much of southern Asia. He certainly left his mark. I remember once reading that such were the great Mongol leader's insatiable appetites, that one out of every 200 men alive today is related to him. I look around the cabin, but it's hard to tell. They're all asleep.

As we draw closer to Beijing, a thickening cloud base obscures the magical, mysterious desert and our long descent is through a daytime darkness, which doesn't let up until the ground appears right below us. Before we know it we're thumping onto the tarmac.

We're met by Nick Bonner, who has led the way in North Korean tourism and whose company Koryo Tours has assembled our itinerary. Neither ITN, with their record of investigative journalism, nor Channel 5 must be mentioned. Both are seen as tools of the British government, therefore lackeys of the Americans etc., etc., though as I am to discover in these bewildering times, being a lackey of the Americans turns out to be not so bad after all.

Washed and freshly clad, I walk from my hotel down the wide east–west highway that slices through the city. 'Beijing's

Thames', Nick Bonner calls it, except here it's a river of traffic, poisoning the air all around it. The nearer I get to Tiananmen Square and the Forbidden City the thicker the crowds become, and the heavier is the police presence. I'm beginning to feel trapped so I turn round and make my way back. Just off the main drag I find, tucked away between the tower blocks, a small park with twisted willow trees and elaborately painted pavilions with glazed tile roofs.

In Beijing, as anywhere else in the world, there is a mass tourist route and an adventurous tourist route. This peaceful little garden encourages me to stray from the beaten track and return to the hotel through labyrinthine back streets. I'm rewarded with a series of busy little markets with food and tea shops and collections of quite surreal bric-a-brac.

DAY 2

FRIDAY 27TH APRIL

I SLEPT WELL, WITH THE HELP OF TWO MELATONIN AND general exhaustion.

Must set the comforts of the Hyatt Hotel behind me today. Though most visitors fly into North Korea, we're taking the slow road, by overnight train to the frontier city of Dandong, and then onto DPRK rails south to Pyongyang. Despite my fondness for trains I know that the journey ahead, particularly with a frontier crossing to negotiate, will be a test of stamina. Neil the director, Jaimie on camera, Jake his assistant, Doug our sound recordist, and I meet up mid-morning at the Koryo Tours office for a briefing. Our very first shot is my arrival. I shoulder my travel bag, wait for the cue then walk up to the door of the office as if I'd never walked up to it before. As Jaimie's camera follows me, I am once again both traveller and travel presenter, back in that no man's land between real life and storytelling, that I haven't experienced since filming in Brazil seven years ago.

Surrounded by the rich collection of socialist-realist posters and the artwork accumulated in the twenty-odd years he's been visiting North Korea, Nick gives us a foretaste of what to expect, mixing a multitude of cautions with a lot of humour. He can't predict everything we'll experience, but his message is that the trip should be something to look forward to. The advice-filled brochures we're given ratchet up the otherness of where we're going. 'DPRK is a conservative society. Koreans generally dress and behave modestly'; 'Attempting to walk around DPRK without a guide accompanying you could land you and your tour company in trouble'; 'perceived insults to, or jokes about, the DPRK political system and its leadership are severely frowned upon'; and, more reassuringly, 'Koreans eat dog meat as a delicacy, but it is not served to tourists as a rule'.

   The only advice which really saddens me is the one which seems to strike at the very essence of travelling. 'Remember that you could place North Koreans and their families in a difficult situation if you attempt to initiate contact with ordinary citizens.'

   Nick gives us our North Korean visas. They're on separate folded cards. Nothing is entered in our passports, to avoid embarrassment when travelling to countries for whom the DPRK is the devil. It's time to wheel our gear to the station. The oppressive heat is building, though the sun remains veiled by overcast skies. Nick checks his smartphone. The air-quality index is around 220. That's in the 'Very Unhealthy' category. 'Not bad for Beijing,' he says chirpily.

   The first stage of our journey into North Korea begins, rather splendidly, at the multi-towered, pagoda-roofed Beijing

railway terminus. A spacious forecourt is already teeming with fellow travellers. The station clock strikes three to the tune of the old Maoist anthem 'The East is Red', taking me back to my first visit to China in the summer of 1988, when it looked, and felt, very different from the way it does now. Gone are the Maoist overalls and the sea of bicycles, and the slogans that adorn the rooftops are more likely to be ads for toothpaste than political rallying cries.

Escalators carry an unending stream of passengers up to the departure floor. Every seat is taken in the assembly area where we await the platform announcement. The only unoccupied seats are those in a small room off to the side, where for a few *yuan* you can sit in massage chairs which grip various parts of

the body in different combinations and wobble them about. Cautiously, I pay my twenty minutes' worth and sit back. It's a weird sensation. Everyone tries to look as if they're simply relaxing, whereas in fact they know and I know that it's like being strapped to a sackful of live badgers.

As I'm being pummelled by my chair, video screens on the opposite wall play live footage of today's historic meeting between the North and South Korean leaders at the Demilitarized Zone in Panmunjom, where the armistice that partitioned Korea nearly seventy years ago was signed. The handshakes, the smiles, the slaps on the back and the coy tiptoeing across a concrete strip may look corny, but they're evidence of an extraordinary development in inter-Korean relations. I feel, though I can't be sure, that this will only be good for us and our access to one of the most tightly closed countries on earth.

The train is clean and modern, with a stainless-steel jug and what looks very much like a spittoon on the window shelf of my four-berth sleeping compartment. Our sound recordist, Doug, snaps a picture of Jaimie, Nick, Neil and me at the moment of departure. We pull out on time, at half-past five. For hour upon hour there's little to see but an unbroken wall of apartment blocks – the tendrils of the city stretching insatiably into the countryside, before merging again with the tendrils of another city that looks exactly the same.

Late supper. Not a bad meal. Garlic shoots, pork and onions; strong and tasty, with cold Budweiser and Great Wall red wine.

I try to sleep but without much success. Cigarette smoke drifts into the compartment from a group talking loudly out in the corridor. I bury my head in the phrase book.

DAY 3
SATURDAY 28TH APRIL

ANNYONGHASIMNIKKA. NANUN YONGGUKSARAM IMNIDA.
Hello, I'm English.

It's coming up to seven as we approach Dandong and I'm looking out of the train window. Rubbish lies scattered by the track. Ranks of residential blocks, thirty or forty storeys high, surfaced in naked grey concrete, block any wider view. Nothing much to catch and hold the eye. A few minutes later, we slide into a modern, functional, spotlessly clean station, floored in polished grey granite. A sign reading 'Please Stand Firm' is not a propaganda slogan but a safety warning as we prepare to descend the escalator. And it's not the only sign in English. Another exhorts us to 'Safely travel, Orderly travel, Warmly travel'.

Time enough before we embark on the train to Pyongyang to walk down to the river for a last look at China. Dandong's downtown glitters and gleams with chrome and aluminium. Somewhat to my surprise a huge statue of Mao Zedong stands across the square from a state-of-the-art Starbucks. He's leaning forward, clad in a greatcoat, arm extended towards Beijing, his back to the wide river that marks the border with North Korea. The plinth alone is the size of a building.

There are one and a half girder bridges over the river. The complete one, known as the China–North Korea Friendship bridge, was opened in May 1943, the year I was born. The other, known familiarly as the Broken Bridge, was bombed by the Americans during the Korean War and ends abruptly in

midstream. A line of tourists are walking out along it, as far as they can go, stopping at the end to stare at North Korea. On the riverside promenade a group of Chinese women are taking selfies beside the cherry blossom. A long, booming waterfront extends away to the north. To the south, on the Korean side, there is little sign of anything much more than grass and mud.

Back at Dandong station, we climb aboard our North Korean train. It's trim and tidy with white-and-green striped coaches, hauled by a big old Chinese locomotive. We pull out of Dandong and rumble across the river, known as the Yalu to the Chinese and the Amnok to the Koreans, that marks the border between China and the Democratic People's Republic.

It's a slow crossing. A socialist market economy slips away and a largely unreformed command economy starts to emerge between the flashing black beams of the bridge. Once across we are in a very different environment. Instead of cars and shops there are people and bicycles and dusty construction sites. Instead of skyscrapers there are sheds. Activity on either side of the train is modest and the whole place feels sleepy. The platforms at Sinuiju station are deserted apart from soldiers standing to attention as we draw in. Portraits of Kim Il Sung and Kim Jong Il, the Great Leaders, hang side by side, on one wall, neat rather than boastful in size. It may feel a bit of an anticlimax, but we are, at last, in North Korea.

We are confined to 'tourist' coaches and kept out of contact with the locals. For some reason there's one fewer tourist coach today so those making the journey are squashed tighter

than usual: Dutch, Austrians, Brits, Canadians, Chinese. Before we can leave for Pyongyang there will be extensive customs and immigration checks. As these are carried out, tall young women with close-fitting white shirts, black trousers, stiletto heels and ponytails wheel snack trollies onto the platform with military precision.

A squad of soldiers in olive-green uniforms and very wide-brimmed caps come down the carriage, almost comically dislodging each other's headgear as they consult closely with each other about our filming equipment. I'm asked if I have any Bibles in my bag (they're phobic about missionaries) or any guidebooks, maps or American films. I'm learning that a sense of independence is the first thing you give up when you enter North Korea. So far the locals seem alternately suspicious of and fascinated by us foreigners. Hence the

combination of military cross-questioning on the train and laughing girls with snack trollies when we're finally allowed off onto the platform.

There's a metal emblem on the side of the train with a red star shining out above a motif of hydroelectric dams and power cables, but as we pull out of Sinuiju that promise of concrete modernity is replaced by timeless agricultural vistas of ploughed fields and small-scale settlements. North Korea is a predominantly mountainous country. Only 20 per cent of the land is cultivable, so it's left to coastal plains like the one we're crossing to produce vital food supplies. They do so with little sign of mechanisation. Men and women cycle between the rice paddies, or walk by with buckets or baskets. Others

squat down, planting shoots and seeds. Geese occupy freshly flooded fields. Carts are drawn by oxen, muzzled to prevent them eating the precious produce. Every few hundred yards blasts from the engine's horn warn people away from the track, but at the speed we're going there's plenty of time to get out of the way. It's as if the country's moving in slow motion.

The compartment is cramped, with three bunks stacked up on either side, so as soon as we can, we retreat to the restaurant car. This is bright and clean. The food is freshly cooked in a spotless galley and served by waitresses in blue aprons with 1950s air hostesses' hats. There's a fixed menu.

All the dishes are carefully laid out in separate bowls in front of me: cabbage soup, spring greens and onions, chicken, prawn, beef stir-fry, hard-boiled eggs and *kimchi*, the Korean staple, made from fermented cabbage in a spicy sauce. I wash it all down with a cold beer. It reminds me of what dining cars used to be like in England, and can no longer be bothered to be. A feeling of great contentment comes over me as I look out at the Korean countryside. There seems to be a concerted tree-planting programme beside the track. The villages we pass are neat and well kept, though my cynical side has me wondering if that's because they're beside the main railway line.

If I get bored looking out of the window, I can watch a wall-mounted TV screen which plays an assembly of clips of Kim Jong Un, smiling broadly as he inspects rocket assembly lines and fires off ballistic missiles to polite applause.

These are interspersed with an eclectic mix of images – rows of tanks lined up on a beach, starbursts, girls playing violins, a scattering of engineering achievements, recently erected children's sports palaces, holiday resorts and stunning mountain scenery. All set to stirring patriotic music. It's a mixture of the Brit Awards, Last Night of the Proms and an arms sales conference.

As we draw closer to Pyongyang there are the first signs of industry, but industry from an earlier era. Brickworks with very tall chimneys, an occasional warehouse, yards and railway sidings. Bulky housing blocks improved with pale washes of colour. The faces of the Great Leaders, always equal in size, always side by side and neatly framed, smile down from displays, looking avuncular, and about as threatening as a Specsavers ad. Their likenesses are sometimes accompanied by the heraldic

symbols of the regime: a hammer, a sickle and a calligraphy brush. Industry, farming and culture.

It's early evening by the time we reach Pyongyang. Peering out of the window with more than usual curiosity I'm a little disappointed to see a largely conventional modern city, with nothing that immediately catches the eye apart from a futuristic glass pyramid which rises high above the surrounding buildings like something from outer space. I later learn that this is the Ryugyong Hotel, built in 1987 but still, mysteriously, unoccupied. In fact, at over a thousand feet high, it is officially the Tallest Unoccupied Building in the World.

Awaiting us on the platform are my two guides. One introduces herself as Li So Hyang (Li being the family name).

She's in her late twenties, short, pale-skinned and neatly dressed in a skirt and tailored jacket. Her smile and proffered hand make me feel she's done this sort of thing before. The other guide is a slightly older man, Li Hyon Chol, in a suit and smiling too, but with less assurance.

Accompanying the guides but hovering more discreetly in the background are a small gaggle of officials. They represent our hosts, the Korea International Travel Company and the National Tourism Administration. Nick tells me that despite the heavy-duty titles, they are a profit-motivated company. I can't catch any of their names apart from Mrs Kim, a short middle-aged woman who seems to have some authority. The rest are all men. In their identical dark suits and ties, they bear a forbidding resemblance to the cast of *Reservoir Dogs*.

Normally on my journeys these are just the sort of people

we'd avoid. They have agendas. There are things they want you to see, which are not what you want to see, and vice versa. But we know the rules here. There is no such thing as unrestricted access, especially if you're from the West and accompanied by a film crew, and we will probably be seeing most of these people most of the time for the next two weeks.

But we've arrived, and that in itself is something of an achievement. We have not been stopped from filming as we emerge from the train, and no one has objected to Jaimie discreetly swinging his camera away from us to pick up some valuable glimpses of platform life. Parents meeting children. Couples reunited.

And Pyongyang station feels somehow familiar. With its ornate octagonal clock tower and stone-columned colonnade, it's not unlike something you'd find in Europe. Our 'minders' escort us to cars waiting in the forecourt. So Hyang is the only one who can pull off a natural smile. The others do their best, but in their eyes there is only anxiety. We are, after all, as much an unknown quantity to them as they are to us. This is my first glimpse of the streets of Pyongyang. There are cars about, but fewer than you'd expect and for a capital city on a Saturday night everything is markedly un-frenetic. It's a short ride to the hotel, but enough to register the dimness of the street lighting and the absence of any advertising hoardings.

Our hotel is called the Koryo, one of the ancient names for Korea. It comprises two forty-storey towers, bridged halfway up. Inside, the design is bland and modern. But then pretty much all of Pyongyang is modern. It was bombed flat by the Americans in the 1950s. Of the old city, I'm told, only one house remains.

We've been travelling for the best part of twenty-five hours since leaving Beijing, and with our camera equipment impounded in a hotel room for customs clearance, there is nothing more we can do but enjoy the delights of the hotel bar. Not easy at first to get served as the entire staff are glued to screens running and re-running the meeting between the North and South Korean leaders. What is striking from the footage is the ease with which Kim Jong Un presents himself. He seems very much the man in control. Rolling like a Cromer fisherman, smiling broadly, hand extended, exuding chumminess. You would think from his body language that the leaders were old buddies, rather than two men representing mutually exclusive systems who had never met each other before.

The North Korean newsreader comes on. She is a regal figure, middle-aged, quite stout, and wearing national dress, a doll-like outfit with a sash tightly drawn across her chest. She's known locally as the Pink Lady. She sits behind a desk and delivers the news with authoritarian immobility, with no inter-cuts or changes of camera angle.

She may not personify excitement but there's no doubt from her voice that this meeting in the Demilitarized Zone is being seen as a defining moment. Everyone is agog. No one can quite believe what they're seeing. And all we want is a beer.

DAY 4
SUNDAY 29TH APRIL

A LOW RESONATING VIBRATION. A LONG-DRAWN-OUT CHORD that seems to be coming from everywhere around me. It's an eerie, ethereal, synthesised sound – like something Brian Eno might have created. I check the clock. It's 6 a.m. I turn over, pull the blanket over my head and try to ignore it. But there's no escape. The sound is everywhere. Not particularly loud, but eerily insinuating and impossible to ignore. I swing myself out of bed and peer through the curtains into the pale dawn light.

Across the street are three high-rise blocks. They look grey and ghostly. No lights are on. There is no traffic at all in the street, twenty-five storeys below. No sign of a human being, anywhere. The growing awareness of where I am, in a country that has for so long been on everyone's hate lists, begins to nag away at me. The mysterious soundtrack, the grey and lifeless buildings – it all seems to fit a nightmare pattern. Last night's welcome seems a world away.

After a few minutes the music stops. I slip into an uneasy sleep. An hour later it starts again. I throw back the blankets and look out of the window again. The grey walls stare back.

At a quarter to eight I'm up, dressed and ready for work when I hear the knock on my door. It's the film crew, reunited with their equipment and ready to do a quick introductory piece before our supervisors arrive. To my relief, I find I'm not the only one freaked out by the invisible music. The silence of the city is more easily explained. It's Sunday and early on a Sunday most cities are asleep. Funny where the mind can take you, building up a sinister scenario based on prejudice alone.

The menace dissipated, we film a piece to camera – a first impression, which rather settles me down – then to breakfast,

a longish journey, which involves going down to reception, walking to another lift and riding up to the fourth floor of an adjacent tower. The dining room is surreal: an enormous white chamber of banqueting proportions, lit by a constellation of lights shining from a grid on the ceiling. Size does not necessarily mean abundance. The buffet is thin, we're limited to one cup of coffee each, and there are only two other guests there.

At one end of the room is a large painted panel of a lake and a mountain view. I shall see this again, many times. It is Mount Paektu, Korea's tallest and most sacred mountain, hard up against the Chinese border in the far north of the country. One of the only images to be allowed to share wall space with the Great Leaders.

We assemble for the day's filming. This will be the first test of our relationship with Mrs Kim and her team, and already there is a small problem. Neil wants to film me coming out of the hotel and walking to a nearby metro station. There is much discussion among the tourism team. Yong Un, a slim man in his thirties, with dark hair, dark suit and dark eyes, throws troubled glances. Initially it is agreed that I can be filmed leaving the hotel, but for a hundred yards and no further.

Negotiations are then resumed and a compromise is reached. I can be filmed going out of the hotel, but then there is a part of the street which for some reason is out of bounds. Once beyond that, filming can be resumed. I later learn that a department store is being rebuilt and they were unhappy that the mess of the construction site would reflect badly on the city. Once the store was completed they would have had no problem. An early intimation of just how important appearances are to our hosts.

I can only hope it's just a matter of getting used to each other. Like the North–South handshakes on Friday, hosting a Western film crew for a fortnight is something new for everybody.

Once past the forbidden part of the street, the camera follows me on my way to the nearest metro station, the first stage of my journey to the spiritual heart of the city, Mansu Hill and the monument to the Great Leaders. My immediate impression is of a clean city populated by tidily dressed people in plain, undemonstrative, impersonal outfits. Their clothes are in subdued colours and inexpensive fabrics, but there are the occasional bright anoraks and Western-style backpacks. A woman passes carrying a huge child in a sling

in front of her. One thing that is uniform is the discreet party badge that everybody, man or woman, regardless of status, wears on their left-hand side, over the heart. The badges carry the likeness of the two senior, now deceased, Kims – Il Sung and Jong Il – smiling against a backdrop of rippling red flags. These badges are worn by everyone from the age of fourteen upwards, though it doesn't necessarily denote that they are Party members. Out of a population of some twenty-five million, only two million are full members of the Workers' Party of Korea. I notice that one of my two designated, on-camera guides, Li Hyon Chol, wears two badges, one on his jacket and one on his shirt in case he has to take his jacket off.

There are almost no private cars on the streets but there is a wide range of public transport including two-car trams, buses and a metro system. The Pyongyang metro, which first opened fifty years ago, now consists of seventeen stations. The one we are travelling from is Yonggwang ('Glory'). Above the entrance there is a large and striking propaganda poster depicting a group of idealised citizens – an architect, a soldier, a farmer and a worker with a book held aloft – surging forward, their eyes on some distant socialist horizon.

I have seen no consumer advertising at all. Only ideas are sold here. I go down the broad steps, have my ticket checked by an impassive lady, and step onto the escalator. So far no one has taken a blind bit of notice of us.

It's a long way down to the station platforms. Nick tells me that the reason for this is that the stations were also designed to serve as bomb shelters, though none of our minders will confirm that. But there's certainly nothing drab or functional about them.

The platforms are contained within a highly ornate, floral-themed chamber reminiscent of the Moscow subway, dressed with marble columns designed like plant stems and hung with glass and metal chandeliers fashioned into intricate leaf patterns.

Music plays, as it seems to do everywhere – stirring but not aggressively rousing, the soundtrack of North Korea. Peppermint-green and aubergine coloured trains roll in and out frequently, and I travel a few stops as far as Reunification station. No floral theme here but a more sober reminder of their recent history: a series of bronze relief panels depicting heroic workers, some alongside a tractor, others with drills, and

in one a sad-looking group of Koreans beside a barbed-wire fence on which hangs a sign 'US Army. Keep Out'.

It's an increasingly warm walk from the station up many long, wide steps to the Grand Monument on Mansu Hill. This is dominated by two seventy-two-foot-tall bronze statues. One is of the Great Leader, Kim Il Sung, coat open, arm raised over the city, and alongside him his son, General Kim Jong Il, known as the Dear Leader, wearing an unzipped parka. (This was recently re-sculpted to replace a rather more suave three-quarter-length coat. More man of the people?)

These two guided the destiny of the DPRK for over sixty years, from its inception in 1948 to Kim Jong Il's death in 2011. I've already noticed that there are no likenesses of the present

leader, Kim Jong Un, to be seen. I'm told that's because 'he is still learning'. Maybe it's just that he can't be immortalised if he's still alive.

Behind the Leaders is a mural of Mount Paektu, and on either side of them two intricately carved processions of soldiers and workers: men, women and children marching heroically forward with the red flag of the revolution waving above them. It's a superbly executed piece of perspective and full of idiosyncratic detail. In amongst the teachers and engineers, I find two women looking heavenwards, one of them carrying a chicken, the other a television.

But it's the monuments of the Great Leaders which have brought us here today, along with a succession of jolly,

smiling wedding groups queuing up to be photographed in front of them.

I learn a number of lessons in the next couple of hours. One is that the Great Leaders must only be photographed in their entirety. It is forbidden to show them in part or in close-up. Another is the importance of getting their titles right, either referring to them as Great Leaders or Great Generals or specifically Generalissimo or President for Kim Il Sung and General for Kim Jong Il.

It's also essential, at all times, to maintain respectful behaviour in their presence. When I sat on one of the steps I was told to get up again and there were palpable cries of horror when our director was seen running to fetch a piece of camera equipment. After my first, quite complicated piece to camera, there was much head-shaking amongst the minders and I was asked to do it again. Not for any political or ideological reasons, but because I had a hand in my pocket.

It's in this far-from-relaxed atmosphere that I embark on my first interview with So Hyang. She speaks English well, and is clearly trying to be as obliging as possible, but from the start she is defensive. Not surprisingly, as our five minders are lined up behind the camera, watching every move. I begin by asking So Hyang about the badges with the faces of Kim Il Sung and Kim Jong Il that everybody has pinned on their left breast. Are they compulsory? She shakes her head, dismissing my question. Why should they be? Any of the masses (and she uses the word 'masses' quite unselfconsciously) would want to wear the badges because the Great Leaders are always alive in their hearts.

As I press her to enlarge on her feelings towards the Leaders, I sense increasing discomfort. There can be no speculation or elaboration of the role of the Leaders. That would be to question the 'single-hearted unity' of the country. I try another tack. The Leaders are dressed very ordinarily. Is this deliberate?

She shrugs off the implication.

'They don't want to look special. They are humble and simple.'

And seventy-two feet tall.

The Great Leaders are the heads of the family, she explains. All the love of the people and the love of the country are embodied in them.

I suggest that even the best families have their disagree-ments. Might there not be things which the leaders do which other members of the family disagree with? I realise almost immediately that I have gone too far. Quite a long way too far. So Hyang shakes her head and looks away in embarrassment. The interview is terminated. There is no direct confrontation over my impertinent question. No one must lose face. Instead our tour company minders call the director across and they go into a huddled discussion.

The interview is not resumed. So Hyang looks shy and apologetic and I'm apologetic too. I just didn't expect the curtain to come down so definitively and so early in the process.

It's hot now, there's no shade or shelter, and I'm beginning to find this triumphal arena oppressive. I feel frustrated, and regret having unwittingly put my guide into such an uncom-fortable position. I hope that the frowns and headshakes from her bosses will not spell problems ahead.

In the afternoon we visit another of the city's landmarks, the Juche Tower. Like everything else of significance here, it embodies the devotion of the people to their leaders by identifying with them in some almost mystical way. In this case, the tower is built with the same number of stone blocks as the number of days Kim Il Sung had then spent on earth. Built in 1982, it rises 500 feet above the city and at its summit is a huge red moulded flame representing the burning torch of the revolution.

The tower dominates the east bank of the Taedong, the river that divides Pyongyang, and lines up with the vast spread of Kim Il Sung Square on the opposite bank. On the local map it

is described as the Tower of the Juche Idea. Juche (pronounced Ju Chay) is the name for the philosophy on which Kim Il Sung founded the DPRK; put simply it means self-reliance, the need not to need anybody else.

And here we get into *Life of Brian* territory. It is only through submitting him- or herself to the revolutionary struggle that an individual can fully realise his or her own self-worth. ('We're all individuals! Yes! We're all individuals!') And this revolutionary struggle must be guided by the Leader, who is the embodiment of the interests of the masses. It may sound contradictory to our ears but understanding Juche is fundamental to understanding North Korea. In a secular country which confiscates Bibles at the border it is the nearest thing to a faith.

A lift carries us up to the top of the tower. It takes a while and on the way I try out my few words of Korean on the lift operator, bedecked in national dress. It's not an easy language. 'Hello' is almost a sentence long. '*Annyonghasimnikka*,' I try, but it comes out most unconvincingly. She doesn't give me a response until my fifteenth attempt when I am rewarded with a big smile and 'Yes. Very good' in perfect English. At the top we step out onto a narrow observation platform beneath the flame. It's the perfect place to be on our first day. The whole city of Pyongyang lies spread out beneath us. Unlike in Beijing, the pollution is minimal and you can see for miles.

I'm struck by how small and compact a capital it is. And not as drab as it looked from my window this morning. Many of the housing blocks have been painted in one of various washes – green, pink, rose red, pale blue. There's a scattering of futuristic architecture – the sinisterly empty Ryugyong Hotel, for instance, and the low-arched bulk of the Rungrado May Day stadium, which reportedly seats 150,000 people, and is claimed to be the biggest in the world.

Out on the viewing platform another motherly figure in national costume greets me and embarks on a well-polished tour-guide routine. Unfortunately her outfit is of light and fluffy material and the wide bow on the outside is no match for the wind that scours the tower. As she talks the ribbon gradually unravels. She bravely tries to re-tie it whilst explaining the Juche philosophy to me in impeccable, doggedly dogmatic English, a process that feels like some mad game-show challenge. The most palely critical of my questions are batted away with unequivocal assurances. There is no one, no one in the

entire country, who does not adhere to the Juche ideology. As with the more defensively adamant attitude with which So Hyang dealt with my questions this morning, this lady feels there is nothing to discuss. Everything is simple. Everyone smiles. There is no room for doubt. In fact there is no room for anything much on the top of the Juche Tower, and when the next lift disgorges a tightly packed group of tourists, I fear for the security of the balcony. Everyone squeezes in around us, among them some loud, brashly confident Chinese from Shanghai and a nice man from Brighouse in Yorkshire.

After a day of landmarks and ideology, it's a relief to accompany So Hyang and Hyon Chol on an early evening walk through a small park and recreation area beside the river. It provides a cluster of high-rise residential blocks with space to exercise, and people have come here after work to stroll

about and watch or play games. Volleyball is the most popular participation sport in North Korea, and So Hyang tells me she plays regularly with a group of friends. I notice that smoking is far more common here than it is back home. I ask So Hyang if she smokes. She shakes her head. 'Smoking is not culturally acceptable for women', she replies, rather primly. Nor, apparently is any overt display of bare skin. This she talks about quite comfortably. She's a modern woman, she dresses to look good, but she also accepts the prevailing view that the West is far too obsessed with bare flesh.

I'm glad that we have this down time together. I have the feeling that So Hyang and Hyon Chol have a different approach to us from that of our minders. Their job is to be as friendly and welcoming as possible, whereas the minders, who are also their employers, must be as suspicious as possible. So Hyang and Hyon Chol are not, I sense, comfortable with the dogmatic way propaganda was served up by the ladies on the Juche Tower. They want to be more relaxed with us but they have to get to know us better first. We end up at a shooting gallery, where they enjoy my limited competence. So Hyang's even worse than I am, and very happy to laugh about it. After a day of carefully crafted propaganda it's a tacit admission that not everything has to be perfect in the DPRK.

Just before I go to bed I take a long look at the night-time skyline. Beneath a full moon, the red flame atop the Juche Tower, cleverly lit from within, flickers away, high above the city, reassuring the inhabitants that the revolution is safe, and they are safe too.

DAY 5

MONDAY 30TH APRIL

SIX A.M. A LOW VIBRATING HUM SEEPS INTO MY subconscious, which slowly becomes my conscious. I walk like a zombie to the window, and still can't pin down what the sound is, where it's coming from. I return to bed. Weird dreams that I'm in North Korea.

Later. I *am* in North Korea, and making the long trip to the breakfast hall. Nick is already there, tucking into an omelette. The mystery of the morning music is explained. He tells me the sound that wakes us is a patriotic anthem called 'Where Are You, Dear General?' which evokes the Great Leader Kim Il Sung.

Music is regarded as a very important element in party unity, broadcast from speakers across the city to motivate the masses, which is why it starts so early, and resounds across the city every hour on the hour until people are at work.

After breakfast, we climb aboard our unit bus accompanied by our two official guides. Old age is revered here. With retirement age in the DPRK at sixty for men and fifty-five for women, anyone still alive in their mid-seventies is treated with respect bordering on the devotional. So Hyang takes my arm and helps me up the steps into the bus. 'Are you tired?' she asks, with concern. As it's only 9.15 in the morning, my response is a little on the brusque side. She nods sympathetically.

'I will be like your daughter,' she says.

After a short journey on traffic-free roads our little convoy pulls into the forecourt of a large school, beside an AstroTurfed

sports pitch. At the main entrance a van is delivering soy milk for the school break. Above the door is another of the framed twin portraits of the Great Leaders, and once inside there they are again, this time in a mural, standing amongst tidily uniformed schoolchildren, surrounded by chunky twentieth-century computers. No flat-screens here. Not yet.

The middle-school pupils I'm here to meet are all in their mid-teens, and clearly primed for a visit. As I'm introduced by their teacher they sit upright at their desks, all in Persil-clean white shirts and all bearing the red badges of the Children's Union. They greet me in English, which, I learn to my surprise, is a compulsory subject for them. They're well drilled, and spirited. I produce a blow-up globe like the one I've taken on many of my round-the-world travels, and as I puff it up with exaggerated effort, they urge me on with each breath. 'One! Two! Three! Four! Five!' until at 'Ten!' the world is inflated.

The globe had been a source of contention earlier as Mrs Kim, having asked to see it first, noticed that it showed Korea as a divided country. The official line here is that, as there has been no officially agreed conclusion to the civil war of the 1950s, South Korea should not be seen as a separate, sovereign country. The problem was eventually solved by inking in the whole of the Korean Peninsula with a Sharpie.

We end up bouncing the world around the class, as each one who catches it calls out the name of a country, and throws it on. It gets quite fast, veering on the out of hand, but there's enough humour in their responses to give me hope that they're not simply programmed to please. Q and A, however, meets with mixed success. 'What other countries would you like to visit?' is on the borderline of controversial and I sense eyes flicking to the teacher before any response. No one says Great Britain, and when I ask if anyone has heard of the Queen every head shakes emphatically.

I ask some of them what they want to be when they leave school. They opt for mostly safe choices – engineers, scientists, soldiers, teachers – but one girl declares that she wants to be 'a famous writer'. I ask what she's written and she stands up and recites a poem. I can't understand exactly what it's about, but the passion and intensity of her delivery are very powerful and there are tears in her eyes and mine as she finishes.

I'm a touch disappointed to be told later this impressive outpouring of emotion was ideologically driven, the poem being a paean to the founder of the republic, Kim Il Sung, and to Paektu, the sacred mountain, where he's said to have taken refuge to organise resistance to the Japanese, who occupied Korea from 1910 to the end of the Second World War in 1945.

From emotional high pressure to physical high pressure in the sports hall, where I witness thrilling table-tennis skills. Some twenty tables in action, and no time for ambling amateurism. Table tennis here means never having to say you're sorry. The players, in their early teens, move with springy athleticism. The air is full of squeaking soles, and shrieks of concentration as the balls fly like bullets.

Is this a show school? Undoubtedly. But I don't feel that once we've gone the tables will be taken away and the all-weather sports pitch will become a police car park. Even if just one school in Pyongyang is equipped like this, it's impressive.

Our hosts and supervisors have laid on a lunch for us in a mock yurt, decorated with plastic flowers, shiny ornaments, PVC strip-curtains covering the doorway and lots of soft toys lying around. Yesterday on Mansu Hill So Hyang made the analogy of the country as a family, with the Great Leaders as father figures, and I sense that the masses are treated almost as children. That, at least, might explain the design aesthetic of primary colours and playground shapes that seem such a feature of the interiors of public places.

The creative hub of Pyongyang is the Mansudae Art Studio. Its status is underlined by a Hollywood-style arched entrance

with decorated iron gates. Beyond it, a service road leads off into the distance, flanked by workshops, offices and production buildings. This is a massive state enterprise, employing a thousand artists who produce everything from paintings, carvings, prints and propaganda posters to the many statues dotted around the city. The Grand Monument to the Great Leaders was designed and constructed here. As there is no commercial advertising in North Korea, all creative energy is directed towards the glorification of the regime. There is no sense of embarrassment about propaganda. It's seen as a perfectly legitimate way of publicising the achievements of the party and the revolution, and it brings all art forms under its umbrella.

In one studio an ex-railwayman, who apparently came late to painting, has almost completed a socialist realist canvas of fishermen at work, bringing in the catch. It's carefully detailed,

technically very skilful and has an energy which fulfils what I assume is its purpose – to inspire and celebrate the fishing industry of the DPRK.

In a nearby studio an equally accomplished artist, this time a sculptor, is at work. He's a fit, grey-haired, rather distinguished-looking eighty-year-old who worked on the gigantic Great Leaders' statues.

Further down the corridor, a slight, studiously bespectacled man of late middle age works away in his studio, crouched on a small stool. He's delicately applying the finishing touches to a poster on which hands from North and South Korea are clasped together, below the words 'Our Nation'. Two microphones on either side of the painting represent the power of dialogue. He

tells me it's not prompted by the recent handshake between Kim Jong Un and South Korean President Moon Jae-in but by Kim Jong Un's New Year message, which set off the current round of rapprochement.

For him, a poster must give 'encouragement and inspiration to people. It should make you feel emotionally connected'. And it should be done whilst the message is strong. Posters are 'urgent works of art. You have to do it quick'.

Some of them are fierce and often shockingly anti-American. One imagines they must be created by angry, bellicose zealots, but this elderly propagandist could not be more gentle and modest. As far as I can tell, the atmosphere of the Mansudae Studio is driven by artistic skills as much as by national rage. Or is it just the people they've chosen for me to meet?

I don't have to agonise over political issues at my next port of call. A stark concrete exterior gives a totally false impression of the pleasure palace that awaits inside the Changgwang Health Complex. In the pillared and domed central hall, the walls and floors are tiled in marble. Coloured fountains welcome you with a play of changing lights. There is an Olympic-sized swimming pool and steam issuing from heat-treatment rooms.

My eye is taken by a beauty salon and barber's shop combined. On the way in there is a wall chart showing the fifteen approved haircuts. North Korean men are directed to keep their hair shorter than five centimetres, unless they're bald, in which case a comb-over is allowed. All of the styles, displayed largely in profile, seem to be exactly the same:

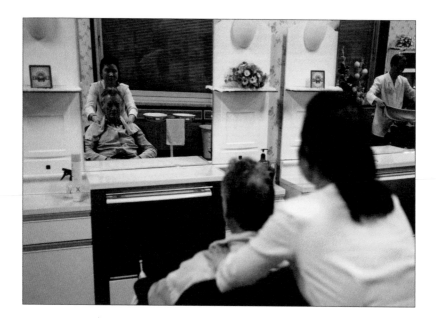

short-cropped and tidy. None of them, I notice, dares to resemble the distinctive basin cut of the current leader.

The salon itself is a crescent-shaped room with basins, mirrors and a row of adjustable chairs, manned, or rather womanned, by formidable ladies in white coats. They will dispense just about anything you want done to your head, short of a lobotomy. I opt for a massage which is duly delivered by a stern lady with steel fingers. Though it's administered as if it might be a punishment, the overall effect is quite the opposite, soothing me into the most comfortable state of relaxation I've experienced since my arrival in Pyongyang.

The day is spilling into night as we descend on a Korean barbecue restaurant for *bulgogi*, which is pork or beef grilled over a fire of hot coals, stoked and delivered in a portable grill which is slipped into a section cut into the table. The red-hot braziers, often with flames licking up from inside, are carried around at arm's length by the waitresses, giving the restaurant more than a passing resemblance to a blacksmith's forge.

The meat, with accompanying prawns, is tasty, and rice and *kimchi* and various sauces are served on the side. To drink, there is a choice of whisky (a Korean favourite) at the bar, *soju*, the local rice wine, and beer from the Taedonggang Brewery which, a few years ago and before the latest round of sanctions, imported its equipment, lock, stock, but not barrels, from the old Usher's Brewery in Trowbridge, Wiltshire.

It's a small, friendly restaurant with family groups at tables. So Hyang and Hyon Chol, relaxed and off duty, are good company. I sense that tonight they have been given licence to enjoy themselves. As I think have Mrs Kim and the

ever-present ring of minders. They've given up monitoring all we talk about, and taken to the bar.

By the time I'm back on the twenty-fifth floor of the Koryo Hotel it's midnight. I feel as if I've been here three weeks rather than three days. We've worked hard, but no one's complaining. We're all still intoxicated with the strangeness of North Korea.

DAY 6
TUESDAY 1ST MAY

IT'S MAY DAY IN THE DPRK – INTERNATIONAL WORKERS'
Day – and the country is on holiday. Sadly the sunshine that
has softened our surroundings since we arrived has been
replaced by an un-festive greyness.

Our minibuses head north-east out of town. Leaving the
city behind, we pass through thick woodland in the midst of
which we glimpse an impressive towered and arcaded building.
This, we are told, is the Kumsusan Palace of the Sun, where lie
the embalmed bodies of Kim Il Sung and Kim Jong Il. I cross
a small red line with So Hyang by referring to the legacy of
these men in death. Death, she corrects me, is not a word that
can be applied to the Great Leaders. 'To the Korean people
they are not dead – they are alive in our hearts.'

Crossing a bridge over the Hapjang river, one of the tribu-
taries of the Taedong, the road leads to the slopes of Mount

Taesong, home of the Revolutionary Martyrs' Cemetery, where hundreds of those who fought against the Japanese are buried, each gravestone bearing a bronze bust of its occupant.

It's also the site of the city's biggest amusement park. We disembark and join the rapidly growing crowds, walking up towards a tall decorative arch, beyond which is a Ferris wheel and a very noisy roller coaster on whose ancient frame cars race by with a screeching roar. In front of the arch, a small number of elderly Korean couples, the women in long, billowy national dress, are dancing, formally and carefully, as if in slow motion. This, I'm told, is the Senior Citizens area. I have the feeling that So Hyang expects me to be more comfortable here.

Once beyond the arch, the activity is much less decorous. In an open grassy area, loud, hearty and fiercely competitive games are in progress. Rival teams from various state

companies vie with each other, stirred up by cheerleaders and yelled on by their friends and families. The garment factory in green versus the ball-bearing makers in salmon pink, are engaged in a game in which contestants have to pick up pieces of paper laid out on the ground. On each one is written the name of three things (they could be musical instruments, bottles, articles of clothing, relatives, lunch-boxes, small children) which they then have to collect and carry as fast as they can to the finishing line. The atmosphere is hysterical. One man has had to take his wife. She falls as she runs with him and so intent is he on victory that instead of helping her up he

drags her along the ground for the last hundred yards. I later
see him as one of the contestants in the tug-of-war. Maybe he
was just training.

There is so much spontaneous celebration going on that
our minders are finding it hard to control where and whom
we film. I'm warmly invited to join a dance circle, after which
I walk down past a children's playground where little toddlers
ride, ironically, in ancient-looking tin missiles. Every inch of
grass and woodland is occupied by festive families or groups
of friends, most of whom have a Korean barbecue on the go,
and some are insistent on my joining them. Arms stretch out

towards me, proffering fresh-grilled morsels on the ends of chopsticks, and tumblerfuls of beer or *soju* to wash them down. There's also much dancing to music played at full volume from portable radios the size of small suitcases. I'm pulled into the ring by both men and women and at one point have a wreath placed on my head by the grandfather of a picnicking family. It turns out he's had more than a few *sojus* and some of the younger members of the family usher him away from our camera disapprovingly.

It's quite a liberating day. I'd expected more supervision, more self-consciousness and more mistrust of ourselves and our cameras. But the revels are unforced and uninhibited in a way which smacks of much greater freedom than I'd expected to see in the Hermit Kingdom. And they'll go on late into the night.

Another surprise is that there have been no great military parades to celebrate May Day. The vast expanse of Kim Il Sung Square is deserted as, towards evening, we walk across it on our way to a half-hour river cruise. From the water Pyongyang looks impressive, with her iconic buildings all floodlit and a fine display of dancing fountains, rising, falling, surging and sweeping to the most patriotic music I've heard all day.

DAY 7
WEDNESDAY 2ND MAY

NEIL, OUR DIRECTOR, HAS BROUGHT WITH HIM A CAFETIÈRE and an apparently endless supply of Marks & Spencer's ground coffee, which is doing a great job of boosting morale and augmenting the relatively lean breakfast of omelette, sliced apple and white toast. None of the staff in the breakfast ballroom seem to mind our flagrant violation of the one-coffee rule.

Today we're leaving Pyongyang for the first time, taking the Reunification Highway south to Kaesong. The idea of a united Korea is taken very seriously by the North, and it is magnificently symbolised by the Reunification Arch on the outskirts of the capital.

Modesty of size and design is not a Korean trait. If a statement needs making it needs making big, and this is unlike any arch I've ever seen. Two huge concrete maidens in wide skirts, representing North and South, stretch across to meet each other, nearly a hundred feet above the road, their extended arms holding aloft a stuccoed roundel bearing the outline of a united Korean peninsula. It was erected in 2001 to symbolise President Kim Il Sung's hopes of bringing the two halves of the peninsula together. The emptiness of the road that runs beneath it is a testimony to hope unfulfilled.

Only a week ago there was a serious accident on the Highway. Over thirty Chinese tourists were killed when their coach left the road and overturned. Kim Jong Un was quick to be

photographed commiserating with survivors in the hospital, something that was noted by foreign observers as a rare example of the Korean leadership reaching out rather than covering up.

There's not much to see along the way today. Other vehicles go by every five minutes or so. There are few birds or animals or habitation of any kind to be seen. Treeless agricultural land stretches away on either side of the road, dotted with farm workers moving slowly through the fields. When a sharp shower whips in across this exposed landscape they huddle together for protection against the driving rain.

Being so close to the border with South Korea, Kaesong, just over a hundred miles from Pyongyang, was spared the Allied bombing that flattened the rest of the north in the early 1950s. Now it's the oldest and least damaged city in the whole of Korea, the only settlement that has real history.

The best-preserved complex of buildings in the town are part of what used to be the Songgyunwan Academy where Korean aristocrats came to be educated in the Confucian tradition, which prevailed for 600 years.

I meet up with a local guide and historian in a serene courtyard, linking a series of long, low buildings with traditional upturned-boat shaped roofs, tiles spilling down over the curved corners, supported by stout beams, painted with dragons and lotus flowers. In the grounds there are fine gingko and zelkova trees, some of which date from the time the university was founded. It's a gentle, contemplative place. At the moment there's nobody here but ourselves, and a woodpecker, high up in one of the ancient trees, doggedly hammering away.

The guide tells me that over a thousand years ago, Koryo, as it was called, was a Buddhist kingdom, and there is evidence that human habitation began long before that. Remains have been dated back 30–40,000 years when people from east and north-east Asia settled in the peninsula. By the end of the first century BC the various warring tribes had coalesced into three kingdoms, the northernmost being the Koguryo, who established a capital in Pyongyang in AD 427. Chinese influence had always been strong. The Buddhist religion was introduced via China and later Koreans absorbed Confucian teachings in their schools.

I've been very much aware of how self-contained this country is, with a narrative that seems only to go back seventy years to the founding of the DPRK. So when I ask my guide if past history means anything to the North Koreans, her reply comes as a rather welcome surprise.

'We can learn a lot of lessons from our history,' she is quick to tell me. 'If we know the history then we can accept our mistakes and learn from our weaknesses.'

Though quiet on this wet May morning, the academy is a popular draw for local tourists who want to see what the old Korea looked like, and outside the weighty wooden gates is a shop and post office staffed by women in what we would call folk costumes standing at attention behind glass cabinets full of tourist artefacts. Spoons and chopsticks, jade-green celadon pottery as well as T-shirts and posters, and most popular of all, postcards reproducing the posters. Carousels are stacked with these classic items of propaganda, many of which depict the wrath that would be wreaked upon the Americans by the

North Korean forces should they step out of line: graphic images of GIs being bayoneted, rockets smashing into the Capitol Building, the Statue of Liberty being dismembered.

Our director has an idea that one way of covering this particularly violent manifestation of anti-Americanism would be to film me buying one of these postcards and posting it to an American friend. He suggests Terry Gilliam.

We take a while to set up, and once the camera is running I duly approach the postcard carousel, only to find that the card I was going to pick out is no longer there. I reach for an alternative, only to find that it isn't where it used to be either. In fact I can't find any of the postcards in their original positions. Then, out of the corner of my eye, I notice the nattily suited manager of the shop swiftly removing the remainder of them and handing them to the smiling be-robed lady who swiftly secretes them under the counter. The Basil Fawlty-ish blatancy of the operation leaves me speechless. Neil shakes his head and approaches our minders. What is going on here?

Mrs Kim, Yung Un and the rather more forbidding 'Tall Li' – hooded eyes, glasses – take him aside for one of their discreet discussions. The upshot is that in view of the recent announcement of President Trump's acceptance of the Supreme Leader's invitation to meet for talks, it has been decided that selling postcards of GIs being garrotted and the White House smashed to pieces is no longer in the national interest. They suggest I send my friend some other memory of the DPRK, like a nice bird, or a view of Mount Paektu?

In the end I have to content myself with sending Terry an image of a red star and the shining face of a happy child. This will surely mystify him.

We're to spend the night at the Kaesong Folk Hotel. It's a lodging that aims to attract both North Korean and foreign tourists by playing heavily on the traditional, with a rabbit warren of rooms around small courtyards. A stream crossed by quaint bridges, more scenic than functional, runs through the place.

Before dinner, they lay on folkloric activities – singing, dancing and one that's new to me, rice-pounding. This exercise in ritual humiliation involves my two guides and me wielding massive mallets to pound a lump of dough so that it can be loosened up and used to make rice cakes. The dough is soon so congealed that it's almost impossible to raise the mallets without putting your back out, which seems to be the point.

The chefs stand by stony-faced. They've seen this happen so often they don't even laugh any more.

Dinner is a curious affair, taken in a room almost empty except for a thousand small pots. My room turns out to be quite ample; a lot of bamboo – bamboo mat, bamboo blinds, bamboo hangings around the door. It has painted panels, trees and flowers and lovingly executed calligraphy in the Japanese style. Could it be a nod to the legacy of the Japanese occupation of Korea, such a dominating feature of the first half of the last century?

DAY 8
THURSDAY 3RD MAY

I SLEEP WELL ON A TATAMI MAT WARMED BY *ONDOL,* an underfloor heating system which, like the Roman hypocaust, uses hot air from wood fires beneath the tiles. Peeping through the side of my bamboo blind I see that the weather has turned infinitely more promising for today's journey to the North Korean side of the Demilitarized Zone.

I'm told the man that I shall be speaking to – a North Korean military officer – will be there to answer questions about anything I care to ask, which promises to make our encounter very different from those I've been allowed so far. This could be a rare chance to talk politics.

We all gather at the hotel reception. Things are easier with our minders now. We eat with them in the evening. We see them on the bus. Though they don't talk to us much while we're working, they are beginning to emerge from their dark-suited uniformity. Mrs Kim is less stern than she first appeared.

She's a maternal lady with one son, and quite teasable. Like us, she and her team are learning as they go, trying their best to understand what we want, and calculating how much they can safely give us. It's a simple equation. The more they trust us, the more we shall be able to see.

This morning the signs are promising. I've been seen openly writing these notes, and dictating into my voice recorder. So far no one has asked to look at, or listen to, anything.

It could be the Kaesong effect. This feels like a comfortable, relaxed town. It's spring, the trees are in blossom, the place is well kept. The people seem happy, and among buildings that are centuries old, it's easy to forget the trauma of the last seventy years. As we climb into the bus to leave, I'm aware that where we're going next is the complete opposite.

The strip of land that divides Korea into communist North and capitalist South is known as the DMZ, the Demilitarized Zone. It was set up by the North Koreans, Chinese and the UN after the armistice in 1953, to replace the notorious 38th Parallel, the old border line, which had its roots in the ideological partition of Korea between the Soviet-backed North and the American-backed South at the end of the Second World War.

In 1950 fighting began in a bitter civil war which both sides blamed the other for starting. The North Koreans took Seoul but the United Nations forces under the command of US General Douglas MacArthur rallied, pushing the DPRK forces back across the border. The Chinese then threw huge numbers in defence of their fellow communists and pushed the UN forces back south of Seoul. Stalemate set in, and it was only after newly elected US President Eisenhower allegedly

threatened to use atomic weapons against the North that the
two sides came to the table, bringing a halt, but not an official
end, to hostilities.

The DMZ is a buffer zone, 2.5 miles wide and running
160 miles from one side of the peninsula to the other. It is
meant to be a weapons-free area, though officers are allowed
to carry a pistol. Two hundred and forty farmers work on the
North Korean side of the DMZ, in what must be some of the
most lethal agricultural land in the world. I ask if the farmers
of the DMZ are specially chosen. Heads are shaken.

'No, just normal farmers.'

This sunny morning the fields and low hills look, if not
idyllic, then certainly healthy. In fact the landscape is almost
entirely man-made. The hills conceal anti-tank ditches, revet-
ments, and until very recently landmines. Huge speakers

used to blast propaganda and martial music at South Korea. I'm told that in the new spirit of detente these were shut down and dismantled two days ago.

As we draw closer to Panmunjom, the village where the armistice was signed, we notice that the road is flanked by tall rectangular concrete columns some five metres high. These I'm told are not for decoration but are primed to be brought down across the road to block any invader. The road and railway links which once connected North and South remain closed.

The North Koreans at the border are courteous and steely at the same time. The room where we all assemble is bare, apart from maps and a screen on the wall. My military guide is Lieutenant Colonel Kim. With a wide-brimmed peaked hat and broad unlined features, he could be any age. He exudes a quiet, confident authority, smiling occasionally, but with the mouth, rather than the eyes, as he begins a briefing.

I learn that what we call the Korean War is known here as the Victorious Fatherland Liberation War. We understand it as beginning in June 1950 when 75,000 soldiers from the North Korean People's Army crossed the 38th Parallel into South Korea. The North Koreans see it as beginning a month later when American troops invaded the North. He doesn't mention that it was a UN force. America is seen as the big enemy, not the rest of the world.

Accompanied by an ever-growing entourage of soldiers and minders, Lieutenant Colonel Kim walks me through some immaculately manicured gardens to a low building where the armistice was signed over sixty-five years ago.

He is absolutely adamant in his view of history. Sitting me at the table on which the armistice was signed, he keeps up an impressive running commentary on the way in which, at every turn, the plucky North Koreans fought and defeated the American warmongers. The armistice was a triumph for Supreme Commander Kim Il Sung; the 'little rabbit' had fought off 'the wolf'. When I try to suggest that the little rabbit had some much bigger rabbits helping him, like China and Russia, for instance, he fixes me with a piercing stare and brushes my comment aside.

'The US Army had an atomic bomb at the time. Our side only had rifles.'

As we move on through the gardens, Lieutenant Colonel Kim points out an impressive monument to Kim Il Sung's signing of a document committing the North to the cause of reunification. He rattles off the statistics. 'The monument is 9.4 metres long symbolising the year 1994; the length of his signature is 7.7 metres to symbolise the date, July 7th; and the monument is decorated with eighty-two magnolia flowers, which are the flowers of our country. They represent his age, eighty-two.'

Symbols like this are so important in the DPRK, as I learnt at the Juche Tower. They're a way of enshrining the Great Leaders in the very fabric of the monuments themselves.

Finally we complete our carefully choreographed progress towards the concrete and glass building which overlooks the line of demarcation. The lieutenant colonel ushers me onto a terrace with a clear view of the narrow strip of concrete between the huts that straddle the line of demarcation. Last

week it became, briefly, the most famous strip of concrete in the world, over which the leaders of the two Koreas shook hands for the first time ever.

Of the seven huts built across the demarcation line, four are managed by the DPRK, three by the UN.

The Americans, Lieutenant Colonel Kim assures me, were hell-bent on trying to demolish the armistice machinery. 'There were 815,000 violations of the ceasefire from the American side until late January 1991,' he details briskly. 'Because the US has been threatening us with nuclear weapons, we thought we were in danger of a nuclear war.'

As we stand on the terrace where the North Koreans still stare into the eyeballs of the enemy, I feel emboldened to

suggest that the military stand-off has cost his country dear. Surprisingly he doesn't bite my head off.

'Yes, in some ways in the past,' he admits, 'but now our Supreme Leader has introduced a policy to improve the economy and improve the standard of living. I believe our lifestyle will be more richer in the future.'

And the rockets and nuclear weapons? 'It was always our policy to denuclearise the Korean peninsula, and the whole world.'

I think he's quite impressed when I tell him that I was here twenty-two years ago (filming *Full Circle* for the BBC). I was on the other side, being given the American view of North Korea, which I remember as much more bellicose than

anything I've heard today. I tell him that I fervently hope if I were to come back in another twenty-two years, this same ground would be genuinely demilitarised. A park maybe, a place where children play and people from both sides of the divide sit and eat and talk together.

'I hope so too,' he replies, and breaks into a rare smile. Maybe it's because he knows I'd be ninety-six by then. Whatever the reason, his response sounds genuine and gives me hope.

We drive back along the Reunification Highway. It's 104 miles from the DMZ to Pyongyang, but only 40 miles to Seoul. So short a distance separates the capitals. So vast a distance separates the minds.

DAY 9

FRIDAY 4TH MAY

ON THE DAY WE LEAVE TOWN WE HAVE AN UNWANTED problem of our own. While squeezing his six-foot-plus frame into a very small Pyongyang taxi to shoot the city after dark last night, our cameraman Jaimie strained his back. He then compounded the damage when he choked on a bit of apple coming down in the lift and put his back into spasm. It couldn't have been a worse moment for it to happen as we are about to embark on the cross-country road from Pyongyang to Wonsan.

The Reunification Highway is as smooth as an ice rink compared to the Wonsan Road – 124 miles of decomposing concrete slabs, between which gaps have opened up and been left to swell. The ride is accompanied by a symphony of bumps, bangs and jolts, uncomfortable for anybody at the best of times, but for Jaimie a slow torture. Fortunately his

hard-worked assistant Jake is able to take over and film what develops into a bit of a visual treat.

Once out of Pyongyang we pass through a landscape of spiky granite outcrops fringed with pine trees, the southern ends of dense mountain ranges that stretch all the way up to the northern border with China. Beautiful to look at, but a physical reminder of how mountainous a country North Korea is and how squeezed its arable land.

We stop for lunch at a small hotel and restaurant beside a reservoir. The water glitters in the sun and jagged peaks rise around us, more North Italy than North Korea.

On the last lap to Wonsan truckloads of uniformed soldiers pass us going the other way. From what I understand these are militia men and women setting off to work on the land. Which goes some way to explain the extraordinary statistic that the DPRK has the fourth-largest army in the world, comprising around a quarter of the population. Clearly they're not all on armed alert. Not only farm labour, but much of construction and transport as well, is worked by the military.

After what feels like four hours in a spin dryer we find ourselves in Wonsan. The Dongmyong Hotel is down by the waterfront. The lobby is sepulchrally gloomy, and heavily net-curtained against the brightness outside. The only light comes from a television screen, still playing and re-playing the meeting of the two Korean leaders.

In theory my room has a fine view of the harbour of this port city, where fishing vessels sidle at anchor in the soft evening sunshine. The pity is that I can hardly see it. The panoramic window is so dirty that it looks as if night has already fallen. When night actually does fall the power supply is meagre. The two dim lamps in the room are shrouded in heavily tasselled Russian-style lampshades, creating the impression that everything is set for a seance.

DAY 10

SATURDAY 5TH MAY

TODAY IS MY SEVENTY-FIFTH BIRTHDAY. AND WOULD HAVE been Karl Marx's two hundredth. So where more appropriate to be than somewhere where socialism is still taken seriously?

It's also one of the busiest days on the shoot and we're to meet in reception at 6.30. At six o'clock, as I'm adjusting to the sharp-angled sunlight edging through a gap in the curtains, the bedside phone rings. It's So Hyang. She informs me that, thanks to the new, improved relations with South Korea, the half-hour time difference between Seoul and Pyongyang has just been abolished. So, it's now half-past six, and I'm late. Turns out I'm not the only one. Even the hotel staff don't know what the right time is, as this small but significant piece of reconciliation was only decided on at midnight.

We head out to film in the main square, just behind the seafront, where a group of matronly women, dressed in white blouses, black skirts and black block-heel shoes are lining up to perform their morning routine.

As rousing music booms out through loudspeakers they snap into a smartly choreographed display of red-flag waving, with occasional, rather cursory, steps to left and right. It's not accompanied by much emotion. Rather like the morning music in Pyongyang, their routine has an essentially functional purpose: to exhort the workers to greater efforts as another working day begins.

Here in Wonsan, there are a lot of workers who need exhorting, as a major tourist development, the Wonsan Special Tourist Zone, is taking shape out on the bay. It covers 400 square kilometres and will include hotel beds for 12,000 people, beaches, pools, mineral springs and, according to the tourist brochures, 'more than 3.3 million tons of mud with therapeutic properties for neuralgia and colitis'.

This massive enterprise has its own airport, which local tourist officials are proud to show us. Kalma airport is every traveller's dream: a bright, fully staffed modern terminal with no other passengers to get in the way. This is largely because there are, as yet, no flights in or out. Its future depends on attracting the Chinese (who comprise 80 per cent of North Korea's foreign tourists) once the attractions – 681 of them, we're told – are open. Ultimately they need the South Koreans too – a bigger potential market than even the Chinese.

The man in charge of the Tourist Zone development sees scope for attracting visitors from even further afield. He and his planners went to resorts in Spain and to Disneyland in Paris to get the most up-to-date ideas. He'd very much like the British to come out here.

It's all a huge gamble, and one can understand why Kim Jong Un is now so anxious to show the smile, as well as the clenched fist. In fact, Wonsan is the face of both. Somewhere in the hills surrounding the town are not just holiday camps and ski slopes but also one of North Korea's biggest missile bases.

There's a beach just behind our hotel which I won't easily forget, because, before we leave, I find So Hyang, still dressed

in her black heels and black business suit, marking out a birthday greeting in the sand.

Today I shall have my first real glimpse of conditions in the countryside. We're to visit a cooperative farm a few miles from the town. The further we get from the city, the more people we see, walking, cycling, or simply congregating by the roadside in front of walls covered with slogans and graphics showing the joys of greater productivity.

After a half-hour's drive we turn off the road and along a track that leads to the cooperative. The ubiquitous patriotic music blares out across the fields, and each plot is marked with red flags. The buildings are brightly painted and well kept. It has been, I'm sure, carefully chosen for our visit.

The farmer I shall be talking to is Mrs Kim Hyang Li, a handsome woman, probably in her early forties. She has a head of dark curls, like so many women here. Her face is lightly weathered and there is a toughness in her stance and a wariness in her eyes.

I'm to be filmed working with her in one of the ploughed fields, weeding and preparing the soil for a crop of corn and chilli beans. The sun is high and hot now, but before we can start there is some urgent discussion going on amongst the minders. They are worried that my being on my knees in a field will send out the wrong message about the state of North Korean agriculture. The call has gone out for some symbol of modernity, but they're having difficulty finding one.

Eventually a tractor is located, well used, its red paint chipped and fading. It's moved carefully into a position where the camera can see it. The farmer and I get to work, crouched down in the furrows, scraping away at what looks like pretty poor earth.

I'm to ask her questions as we work, but it isn't easy as she's more concerned with correcting my hoeing technique. She tells me they have developed new scientific methods of farming which have made it easier for them, though I can't see any evidence to back this up. This year conditions have been good, she says. (In fact, figures for the harvest in 2018 now

show a 10 per cent drop in production.) I ask her about the calamitous famines of the 1990s when North Korea's fragile agricultural system, already reeling from the withdrawal of Russian subsidies after the collapse of the USSR, was struck by drought and floods so severe that hundreds of thousands of people perished (estimates of deaths range from 240,000 to over two million). At the time words like 'shortage' and 'famine' were considered traitorous, and the crisis was referred to as the Arduous March, an evocation of the suffering endured by Kim Il Sung and his resistance fighters during their heroic resistance against the Japanese.

Mrs Kim remains tight-lipped.

'Are things better now?' I ask.

'Yes,' she says. 'Things are better now.'

The director judges that we have enough footage of us working away and we both straighten up. My farming companion is asked how it was having me as a helper. To general half-suppressed laughter her verdict is translated.

'He is unnecessary.'

Which is not really what you want to hear. Especially on your birthday.

We tramp through the fields to her home. This cooperative consists of ten villages, comprising 650 farmers and 1,700 residents in all. Farmers work in teams, set their own targets

and give a portion of their produce to the state. In return they get to own their own houses. Mrs Kim is one of the team leaders and lives in a well-kept, spacious bungalow. As we go in she shows off the vegetables growing in her garden. She's especially proud of the thick-leaved Korean white cabbage, which, she says, makes the best *kimchi*. Her small plot looks to be a far more productive space than any of the co-owned land I've seen, and almost as well kept as the garden around the memorial to the Great Leaders that overlooks the village.

At the door I meet her son, twelve or thirteen years old, I should think. He greets me with a winning smile. I try out my best '*Annyonghasimnikka*' to which he replies, shyly but clearly, 'Pleased to meet you.'

Mrs Kim Hyang Li and her husband have three children: her elder son is an officer in the army, her daughter is a teacher.

Whilst his mother works away in the kitchen, her younger son shows me a collection of family photos in a frame on the wall. Most of the men and most of the boys are in military uniform. I ask him what he wants to do when he leaves school.

'Army,' he says, smiling proudly.

He has some English homework to do and, whilst his mother prepares the meal, I look over his shoulder at the textbook he's using, and we try out words to match the illustrations. 'Clock', 'hand', 'tree'. His pronunciation is spot on.

The house is sparsely furnished and I'm served food sitting cross-legged on a patterned carpet beneath a wall that is bare, save for portraits of the Great Leaders. Hyang Li lays out half a dozen platefuls in front of me – sweet potatoes, persimmon, apples – then sets before me a brimming bowl of soup and *kimchi*.

The minders hum with approval.

She watches solicitously as I eat, giving me instructions every now and then.

'You must finish the *kimchi*.' 'Now drink the soup.' I sense that this is her way of dealing with my impertinent questions about famine and scarcity.

Before we go, there's one last thing she wants to show us. Leading me to the framed photos she points out a picture of her, looking proud as a peacock. 'This is a picture of me receiving fish from Kim Jong Un for doing well at my job.' She turns to me with a radiant smile, all trace of severity gone.

By the time we're back in Wonsan, the sun is setting and we've put in a twelve-hour day. Everyone's desperately hungry, so after a drink in the bar we walk through darkened streets to the modest restaurant we discovered last night.

Frustratingly, the minders are taking an age to join us. Are they debriefing? Checking the material we shot today? It's part of our agreement with them that they can look at the footage.

Eventually they appear. But still no food. They've always been punctilious about making sure we're served promptly, but tonight Mrs Kim, brow furrowed, is in deep conversation with the restaurant manager. There's a palpable sense of crisis.

Then all becomes clear. We are shown into a small back room where a long table is set out, decorated with balloons and tinsel. As soon as we've sat down the formidably dour Tall Li comes in with a huge bunch of flowers which he hands across the table to me. This is followed by what I assume must have been the reason for all the subterfuge, an enormous cake, candled and coated in thick cream and presented to me by So Hyang. Cameras flash and, with faces flushed, they all sing a rousing Anglo-Korean chorus of 'Happy Birthday'. Mrs Kim, smiling anxiously, hands me a present.

I give a short speech. In thanking them all I say that I never really expected to be seventy-five and never in my wildest dreams could I have expected to spend the great day digging in the soil of a farm in North Korea. This has been the most extraordinary and wonderful birthday of my life, only equalled by my thirtieth birthday performing in a Python show at the Birmingham Hippodrome, when the entire audience sang 'Happy Birthday' at the end of the Dead Parrot sketch.

Back at the hotel reception, European Champions League football, the first manifestation of anything from outside the DPRK, has replaced the two leaders on the television. In my room a warm wind is beating against the windows, sucking the

net curtains out and then thrusting them back. It's late, but I'm no longer tired. I arrange my birthday cards on the table, put my flowers in water, and open Mrs Kim's present. It's a book of photos of North Korea.

There are some shouts out in the street, then silence.

DAY 11
SUNDAY 6TH MAY

A RESTORATIVE NIGHT'S SLEEP. THE DONGMYONG HOTEL seems less oppressive this morning. Comfortable bed, abundant hot water and even the toilet-roll ends neatly pointed. The breakfast buffet offers a choice of dishes, among them 'Steamed pollock entrails'. Perhaps another day.

At 8.30 we board our minibus to drive the sixty-odd miles south to Mount Kumgang, which according to the notes I've been given by Koryo Tours, is 'a most beautiful mountain landscape with deep gorges, waterfalls and lagoons which are considered a sacred source of power and spiritual renewal' for the Korean people. There's that word 'sacred' again. I'm never quite sure how it's compatible with state atheism.

As we leave Wonsan, we're into patches of mist and rain. Through the window, a glimpse of children collecting stones from a river bed. A scenic drive, with a railway on one side, and green fields on the other in which I notice, for the first time, livestock in some numbers: small groups of cows, sheep and goats. Beyond them is the coastline of the East Sea, with inlets and fine beaches – tempting, but separated from the road by a barbed-wire fence.

Mid-morning we stop at a checkpoint, not something we've seen much of so far. Whilst papers and permissions are being scrutinised, I wander a little way down the road to take in the sounds and smells of the countryside. I am sharply warned to return to the bus.

Clearly they're more paranoid about security round here. Is it the proximity to the border? Or the ocean? Or do the trees conceal a man-made forest of military installations? The thing about North Korea is that you never really know. About anything.

We move on, passing heavily laden bicycles and carts pulled by muzzled oxen. A team of men are stripping concrete from a bridge using only hammers and chisels.

Our bus's progress is slow and there's plenty of time to talk with So Hyang and Hyon Chol. So Hyang's father is about to retire and is thinking of taking up fishing. Hyon Chol's recently married, but So Hyang remains unattached. She's twenty-eight and by her own admission will be considered to have real problems if she's not married by the age of thirty. She has a tough streak of independence, and I get the feeling she won't be pushed into anything she doesn't want to do. I ask what kind of romantic behaviour is considered publicly acceptable. So Hyang tells me that things have changed. Holding hands used to be disapproved of but is now permitted. 'Kissing?' She shakes her head firmly. 'Never. That's private.'

The closer we come to the DMZ, the steeper and more dramatic is the scenery. Eventually the road peters out and the mountain trail begins. It leads up to Mount Kumgang, a granite peak which glitters in the sunlight and is known as Diamond Mountain. We walk up beside a river bed which, judging by the size of the boulders along its path, must be filled with thunderous water flows when the rains come. Today, it's just damp and cold and the torrent is reduced to a gentle stream. Not as supremely sacred as Mount Paektu, Kumgang has nevertheless always been revered, as is shown by the numerous inscriptions on the rocks we pass on our climb – some in Korean, but others in Chinese script, dating back hundreds of years.

On either side of us are towering outcrops, eroded by rain and wind into heart-stopping, gravity-defying formations.

Some stacks seem to be hanging by a thread. Others have collapsed already and we have to pick our way carefully round the scattered remnants.

Our minders don't look happy at all. This is not their preferred environment, and none of them is dressed for the sharply dropping temperatures as we climb higher. They're like city boys on an Outward Bound course, still wearing dark suits and black leather shoes. They look upwards uneasily, and eventually, when they have reached a point where the path tunnels beneath a rocky outcrop, they decide to take shelter, and leave us to go ahead on our own.

A few hundred yards further on there is a narrow footbridge and below it a huddle of massive white boulders. This offers

So Hyang and me a rare opportunity to talk on camera without being supervised. We scramble down onto the rocks, and having found a suitably eye-catching spot, we pose ourselves, Ruskin-like, and unpack our picnic.

So Hyang opens a picnic box and hands me a sandwich. It feels rather an intimate moment, taking me back to my childhood, evoking memories of school trips up the steep valleys outside Sheffield.

The interview is relaxed, but as soon as anything political is mentioned, her guard is up. She knows that the camera's turning, and that, although the minders are absent, they will still check every foot of the recording. My hope is that if I'm open about the foibles of our leaders she will open up about her own.

'Our way of life is based on freedom of speech,' I say. 'People can be as rude as they like about their leaders. In my country we are able to criticise our leaders if they do something wrong, and like any human beings they frequently do make mistakes.'

So Hyang plays it straight back to me.

'That's what makes us so different,' she replies. 'Our leaders are very great. They are not individuals. They represent the masses, so we cannot criticise ourselves, can we?'

I don't really know where to go with this.

'Criticising our leaders is like criticising ourselves,' she persists.

We fence with each other in this sublime landscape. I'm trying to break down the barriers between us which, frustratingly, are not human but ideological. I know So Hyang to be bright and intelligent. She tells me she has read Jane Austen

and Charlotte Brontë and Charles Dickens, so she must know that other cultures do things differently and that Dickens of all people found much about his country to criticise. But it's no good, she won't be led. It's as if the only thing she'll criticise is criticism itself.

We stay the night at a huge grey hulk of a hotel surrounded by wooded mountains but making not the slightest effort to blend in with them. It was built and financed by an affiliate of the South Korean giant Hyundai, who twenty years ago invested 400 million dollars in developing a resort around Kumgang. Only a few miles from the border, and regarded as an area of great natural beauty, it was seen as a place where Koreans from both sides of the peninsula could be temporarily reunited.

This worked well, attracting over a million South Korean tourists, until the fateful morning of 11 July 2008 when one of

them, a fifty-three-year-old woman, was shot dead while taking an early morning walk. The North Koreans claimed that she had entered a military area. I remembered the barbed-wire fencing by the side of the road on the way here, and how sharply I was warned to get back in the bus when, attracted by the beauty of my surroundings, I too took a walk.

The consequence of the shooting was the immediate recall of all South Korean tourists. They have never returned. Their government has embargoed the area ever since, and the DPRK has lost a considerable source of revenue.

The North Koreans have taken over the running of the hotel but can't do much to make the enormous public rooms look anything other than forlorn. It so happens that tonight, however, we may not be the only guests. There are two coaches drawn up on the forecourt, believed to be a Chinese tour.

DAY 12

MONDAY 7TH MAY

EARLY IN THE MORNING I'M WOKEN BY WHAT SOUNDS like a riot. Raised Chinese voices. Shouts, yelps, occasional shrieks and high-pitched laughter. It's all coming from the corridor outside my room. I check my watch. It's 6.30. I pull the pillow over my head, but further sleep is out of the question. At around 7.00 I hear a distinctly English voice adding to the cacophony. It's Nick Bonner, and he is not happy.

'You are the rudest people on earth!' I hear him bellow from his bedroom door. There is a moment's startled silence, then it all begins again.

By the time we get down to breakfast the hotel is once more shrouded in silence. The two coaches have gone. And Anglo-Chinese relations are, presumably, at a new low.

Around 9.30 we leave the mountains and retrace our steps towards Wonsan. There has been much discussion as

to whether we can crown our North Korean journey with a visit to Mount Paektu. It's over 300 miles to the north and there may be snow and ice to greet us, not to mention security issues. But Mrs Kim and the minders are hopeful and we drive straight to Kalma airport.

Today there is a buzz of activity at the terminal. The check-in desk is open and a lady, as immaculately attractive as the traffic cops in Pyongyang, or the trolley girls at Sinuiju station, is looking at visas and issuing real boarding passes. The airport manager is wielding his radio with a convincing sense of purpose. And all this because today there is a departure on the board. Koryo Airlines flight JS 7301 to Samjiyon, departing 2.30. Samjiyon is a military and civilian airport on the northern border with China, and the gateway to Mount Paektu. So there is hope.

Whilst we wait, we eat lunch at the airport restaurant. It's themed as an aircraft cabin. Like the yurt restaurant in Pyongyang, the design is bright and childlike, as if we're in a nursery for grown-ups.

I've plenty of time for reflections like this as we've now been told that the only departure of the day has run into trouble. The airport manager's expression is fraught as he stares out onto the spotless, plane-less runways in search of our aircraft, which is coming in from Pyongyang. His radio crackles. His expression morphs from anxiety to anguish. There is fog at Pyongyang and the incoming flight has not taken off yet.

Smooth-listening muzak — Verdi and lavish instrumental versions of pop songs — is pumped across the terminal. I hear a wordless version of 'Sealed With a Kiss' about twelve times. Video screens display hyperbolic loops boasting of state successes. 'Scientists' Holiday Park, completed in over four months!' High on the wall a line of panels mark the time in different parts of the world – 'Moscow', 'London', 'Beijing', 'Pyongyang'. One panel is significantly empty. Could it be soon filled by 'Washington'?

To pass the time Neil thinks it might be interesting to show So Hyang something of my previous work. He's brought along with him the Fish Slapping Dance from *Monty Python*. Chin on her arm, So Hyang stares at the laptop with great concentration as John Cleese and I perform our fish slapping with a military precision that North Koreans would surely appreciate. As I'm knocked into the water she laughs loud and appreciatively, though her immediate thoughts are not for the man who's just plunged head first into a canal.

'The fish,' she asks with concern, 'is it alive?'

I reassure her that the fish was dead, but the human was alive.

Around five o'clock there is a burst of radio activity. Forty minutes later, through the clearing mist, the one flight of the day touches down. It's a twin-engined Antonov turbo prop, built in Russia in 1967, and operated by Air Koryo, which, I've been assured by some insensitive soul, has one of the worst safety records in the world. This, I later learn from Nick, was an unpardonable slur. With no fatal accidents and only two emergency landings in several decades Air Koryo actually

have a better safety record than almost any other airline. And I wasn't paid a single *won* to say that.

Once aboard, I feel rather at home. The cabin interior is a throwback to the old days of air travel. No long rows of rigid plastic seats here. Flight JS 7301 has carpets, mirrors and gold brocade wall coverings. The seats, more like small armchairs, have velvet-trim covers. It's like being in a boudoir, rather than at the mercy of some accountant's dream of maximised revenue loading.

We fly due north for an hour. High mountains, dusted with snow, rise to meet us. It's a world away from the beaches of Wonsan. A world of lakes and peaks and pine forests. When the plane touches down at Samjiyon we disembark into a cold and windswept night. Our minders, either macho or misinformed, have only their dark suits to protect them against the weather. After much shaking of heads, Yung Un, one of our minders, and a city boy if ever there was one, reluctantly agrees to take up the offer of a spare anorak I have with me.

A coach has been laid on to drive us to the hotel nearest Mount Paektu. It's a long drive on largely rough, unmade tracks with cleared snow piled up on either side. The forest cover is dense and dark. Pine, larch and fir trees hem us in.

To my surprise there are people out there: dark shapes moving in and out of the trees. Occasionally our headlights pick up figures bending low by the roadside, collecting wood. After a while we're joined by other vehicles on the road: big trucks, pulling out of side turnings ahead of us, frequently bringing our bus to a standstill. Now I can see lights among the trees, and fires burning, and suddenly we're in the midst of an enormous construction site. It may be 8.00 at night, bitterly cold and with darkness falling, but legions of workers are toiling out here under arc lights. They're pushing wheelbarrows, carrying bricks, levelling roads, digging ditches, marking out the foundations of houses. Lines of workers, male and female, pass baskets of spoil from one to the other. This is organised human labour on an astonishing scale in the most unlikely of surroundings.

The hotel we eventually arrive at is low slung and gabled, like a concrete chalet. The freezing cold lobby is dominated by an enormous mural of the Great Leaders in Paektu country, Kim Il Sung in overcoat with arm raised, his son Kim Jong Il beside him in a brown boiler suit. I notice a difference in the

attitude of the hotel workers. In Pyongyang and Wonsan nobody took much notice of us. Up here they just stand and stare.

The word goes out that there is a special potato barbecue being served this evening, but I'm advised to wear a coat and scarf, as it's outside. Further enquiries lead me to a dark corner of the hotel grounds, where a small group of people are huddled around the glowing embers of a fire. Occasionally a scarf-wreathed figure reaches down, retrieves something from the ashes, wraps it in a piece of brown paper and hands it around.

The night is so dark that what I'm given could be a lump of coal, or it could be a dead mouse. It's so long since we last ate that I bite into whatever it is most gratefully. I'm rewarded

with a piece of pure carbon with a soft and tasty potato at its centre. A glass of *soju* is thrust into my other hand.

In the intimacy engendered by darkness and *soju*, I ask Yung Un what it is we passed in the forest. It's a new city, he says, which is being built by one of the Shock Brigades, a term coined in the USSR to describe highly motivated workers with fiercely competitive productivity goals. There is no money for machinery so they have to build these massive developments by hand. These people are not forced to work in these conditions. It is an honour to be part of a Shock Brigade, he says. He himself spent four years working in one.

Despite his reassurances I feel sure that these workers are not here out of choice, and that up here in the far north I'm seeing a glimpse, literally and figuratively, of the dark side of the Democratic People's Republic.

There is one advantage of being somewhere so remote on a night like this. As I tip back my glass of *soju* I look up into the heavens and am rewarded with one of the most piercingly clear views of the galaxy I have ever seen.

DAY 13

TUESDAY 8TH MAY

THANKS TO THE ANCIENT WONDERS OF *ONDOL*, MY ROOM IS very, very warm, whilst the rest of the hotel remains very, very cold. Both bed and pillow are rock hard. There was no hot water last night. We were assured it would be available for a short time in the morning. It wasn't. Well, not at the time we were told, but now it's gurgling out, rather grudgingly.

Breakfast is laid out on plates before us and mostly consists of a potato.

It's a peerless day of sharp, cold sunshine. Too cold, we're told, to contemplate a pilgrimage to Mount Paektu which, at 9,000 feet, is the highest point on the Korean peninsula, and still capped by ice and snow. I'm a little disappointed we can't get closer because Paektu, apart from its significance to

Koreans north and south, is an active volcano – it last erupted in 1903 – and contains within its crater what I'm told is the deepest mountain lake in the world. Its summit, the highest of a cluster of peaks and ridges on the northern horizon, rises behind a soaring statue of Kim Il Sung in his prime. He gazes down on what looks like an enormous parade ground, hacked out of the surrounding forest, as if awaiting some massive demonstration of loyalty and devotion. I recall the poem which the girl recited with such passion at the school in Pyongyang, a translation of which I'd scribbled down in my notebook. I wonder if she had composed it here.

Mount Paektu!
That time I put on my rabbit-patterned bag
I was drawing you with my crayons that day,
Spreading the wings of a young mind.
I climbed to the top.
Oh, the longing that has been accumulating like a mountain,
Pouring on the holy land of revolution.
I am now at Mount Paektu.
Climbing Mount Paektu as I so wished
Bursting out! Bursting out!

My faux pas of the day is to take a photo of the Leader from behind. I want to get an all-round view of the impressive monument, sixty feet high and skilfully sculpted. But I'm sharply instructed to put my camera away and reminded, as I

was in Pyongyang, that any image of the Leaders, apart from full-length, front-on, is considered deeply disrespectful.

Next on the Great Leader trail is the cabin in the woods where Kim Il Sung hid out whilst leading, Che Guevara-like, the resistance to the Japanese occupiers in the 1930s. A neatly paved path leads up to a log cabin with a red flag flying above it. It's a replica of the original humble dwelling where, so legend has it, Kim Jong Il was born in 1941, to the revolutionary leader Kim Il Sung and his formidable wife Kim Jong Suk, also a resistance worker, who was serving as a member of the Sewing Unit at the time.

A female guide in army uniform delivers the tourist spiel, pointing out Kim Il Sung's hat on a peg, a 1930s map of the world, the chopsticks he ate with, the blanket made for their baby. It's all fairly standard stuff until she comes to the

birth of their son, the future Great Leader. Here her delivery goes up a note. Settling her gaze somewhere in the middle distance, she describes the circumstances of his birth in the same manner and with the same intense, almost trance-like quaver as the schoolgirl reciting her Mount Paektu poem. How the weather changed on the morning he was born, and a star and a double rainbow appeared in the sky, and 'all the soldiers believed a child had been born who would lead his people out of captivity!' The equivalent, almost word for word, of what you'd find in a banned Bible.

At various points throughout the forest there are shrines to the Great Leaders, massive marble emplacements bearing poems they've written, a mosaic tableau depicting a youthful Kim Il Sung standing with his wife and child amongst snow-laden pine trees, and there is even a Kim Jong Il Peak, with his name marked out on the sheer rock face, each character inscribed on stone blocks weighing fifty tons each.

The association of the Great Leaders with Mount Paektu is challenged by some historians. Official records show that Kim Il Sung did indeed become a brave and able leader of resistance to the Japanese, but from a base in Siberia, where the Russians trained and taught him, and that he remained in Russia from 1935 until the defeat of the Japanese in 1945.

If that's true, and like so many of the Kim stories it's often impossible to distinguish fact from fiction, then it means that all this relentless identification of the Leaders with Mount Paektu is a fantasy, a deliberately contrived cornerstone of the cult of the Kims, who describe themselves as the 'Mount

Paektu bloodline'. This, of course, is not open to doubt in North Korea. For the official account of their origins to work then everyone has to believe that it is the reality. To ask questions, to debate the facts, to suggest things might have happened otherwise, is disloyal and dangerous. It gives succour to the enemy. And the DPRK's existence, and its undoubted achievements, are all based on the existence of enemies. The Japanese, the Americans, the traitorous capitalists to the south.

Hence the relentless reminders of the presence of the Great Leaders in this remote and inhospitable corner of the country. Do as you're told and above all accept what you're told as the truth.

And don't photograph them from behind.

The fact that we can't make the trek up the mountain gives us little reason to hang around in this inhospitably cold corner of the country, especially as none of the minders have coats, and later in the afternoon we return to the airstrip at Samjiyon. There's a long security hold up, as we have to pass everything through a metal detector. It's only after a while that I notice it's not plugged in. Eventually we're cleared to board our Antonov and head back to Pyongyang. Nearly two hours later, as we descend towards the capital, back amongst low green hills and sunlit valleys, there is a whirring and a rumbling just opposite my window, and I look out to see the comforting sight of the undercarriage creaking down in preparation for landing. Not two minutes later, I look out again to see the undercarriage disappearing back under the wing. I study the faces of my fellow passengers. No one seems to have noticed. Nick, I think, might have seen it too, but like me

didn't want to worry anyone by screaming. Instead, he diverts our attention by pointing out Kim Jong Un's all-white private jet on the ground below. It's a rare sight, according to Nick, and must mean that he has just arrived from somewhere, hence the last-minute postponement of our landing in Pyongyang.

Later – quite a while later – the wheels come down again and this time they stay down. The Paektu adventure is over. Pyongyang, which seemed such a strange place two weeks ago, now feels like home, and I find myself oddly stirred as we drive in from the airport past the magnificent Arch of Triumph, like the one in Paris, but thirty feet taller.

Like the Juche Tower, the Arch of Triumph is a tribute, in masonry, to the founding father of the DPRK. It was completed on Kim Il Sung's seventieth birthday and comprises 25,500 blocks of white granite, each one representing a day of his life. It is him.

DAY 14
WEDNESDAY 9TH MAY

A BRIGHT DAWN. THE WEATHER LOOKS SET FAIR FOR OUR last full day in the DPRK. The phone rings as I'm dressing. It's So Hyang. For a moment I think she might be calling to say that the time difference has been restored again, but her message this time is rather more mysterious. The hotel lobby will be out of bounds for arriving or departing guests for the next half-hour. No reason given. I slip down to breakfast. Nothing seems to be happening and I return to my room thirty minutes later to get myself ready for our last day's filming.

When I emerge from the lift this time I find myself in the midst of a crowd of people, some of them Koreans, but the rest an altogether taller, bulkier race, with American accents and Bluetooth earphones. A blonde woman looks around with a tight, impatient impression and a dark-haired man beside her clutches a thick sheaf of notes. In the middle of the throng is

a burly, heavy-framed man who I later learn is Mike Pompeo, the American Secretary of State. He and his team are here to finalise the repatriation of a number of Americans imprisoned by the regime for so-called 'hostile acts', which had previously included distributing Bibles and spreading Christianity.

Pompeo's arrival in North Korea, which would have been totally unthinkable four months ago, shows just how fast Kim Jong Un's charm offensive is moving. Far from being one of the world's diplomatic backwaters, the DPRK has been the epicentre of international affairs for these past two weeks. And this is another extraordinary chapter. It's not every day you see an American Secretary of State in your hotel lobby. Especially a lobby in the axis of evil.

Our last day is a bit of a whirlwind. At a big, well-equipped sports centre I watch a display of taekwondo, the Korean martial art which is practised here with quite stunning strength, agility and concentrated intensity.

Using a combination of high kicks, twists, and hard, harsh shouts, they demonstrate how to disarm any attacker, after which they take it out on bricks and blocks of wood on which a skilful martial artist can administer a force of 200 kilograms. A slim, young, softly spoken girl, who spends sixteen hours a week training, teaches me the basics. Like standing up straight.

As with the table-tennis players I saw at the school, there is in all things they do a fierce determination to be the best.

Faces are tense and tight-lipped. They are doing it for the Kims, who look down on them from the wall.

We take a mid-morning break at somewhere I wish we'd found earlier. Coffee shops are practically non-existent in the North Korean capital, certainly ones smelling of freshly ground beans. Hence our great delight at finding a café, set up by an Austrian coffee roaster, Helmut Sacher, in partnership with Austrian entrepreneur, Helmut Brannen, who specialises in bringing the finest coffee to the least likely places. They have a branch in Ulan Bator.

The atmosphere is Viennese, low-lit, lampshaded and intimate, with real coffee, whipped cream and cake. It's a small, private space that feels like a welcome contrast to the prevailing gigantism of the city's public spaces. But by coincidence, the two are side by side, because the café is on the corner of perhaps the most well-known of Pyongyang's arenas, the colossal Kim Il Sung Square. This is probably the only corner of North Korea that international audiences might be able to identify, for this is where the parades and marches and displays of military might take place, though most of the time it's used for cultural activities, sports demonstrations and the expertly choreographed mass dances for which the North Koreans are renowned.

Two sides of the square are flanked by grand Stalinist facades but at one end rise the pitched and tiled roofs of an impressive Korean-style building, dating from the 1980s, from whose long balconies salutes are taken in military parades. The building itself has no military purpose. It is in fact the national library, known as the Grand People's Study House.

I look up at the Study House from the vastness of Kim Il Sung Square, feeling tiny in a space that can easily accommodate over 100,000 participants at a time. On the ground are lines of discreet white dots to show exactly where each member of the display stands, and how much room they've got on either side. It's tight.

Our last lunch is at a hugely popular restaurant serving the national dish, *naengmyeon*. Tables are at a premium, for it seems that the people of Pyongyang cannot get enough of buckwheat noodles in an iced broth with half a boiled egg perched on top.

Once you've got used to the fact that they're cold, the noodles are tasty. They're served in great heavy bunches which are not easy to eat politely. My chopsticks have difficulty heaving them off the plate, let alone into my mouth. Consumption is a messy, but ultimately rewarding, process.

It is in this fabled restaurant that our minders ask us for the first time to erase footage that we've shot. And it isn't over any big issue, simply that diners on one table object to being filmed. The rest of the time, although there have been robust arguments about how material might be edited, nothing has met with blanket disapproval. Which is not what any of us had expected.

In the afternoon we film along the extraordinary phenomenon that is Mirae Street, or Future Scientists Street, an avenue of intriguingly designed forty-storey towers that were completed in less than a year. Much of the work was done by soldier-builders, members of North Korea's vast army, working day and night. They describe such swift construction as building at 'Chollima speed', Chollima being a mythical winged horse, co-opted by the regime as a symbol of the speed with which the economy needed to be rebuilt after the war.

The Western view I've often heard expressed is that these tower blocks are merely a grand gesture, a visual shell, empty and unfinished inside. I can refute this suspicion and confirm that at least one family has moved in. On the tenth of forty-four floors I'm invited into a spacious apartment, home to a husband and wife, two children and two grandparents. The grandparents are expected to look after preschool children so both parents can go out to work.

I meet the wife, who happens to be at home today and is happy to show me around. She's in her thirties, I'd imagine,

dark hair neatly styled, and considering she can't have had that many Western film crews in her kitchen, remarkably relaxed. There are a lot of artificial flowers and stuffed toys around and an air-conditioning unit called 'Enjoy Wind'.

This apartment is in a street for the elite, a concentration of top scientists and university professors, reaping the reward no doubt for creating the nuclear weapons that allow this small country to punch so far above its weight.

It's early evening as we leave the towers of Mirae Street. At ground level there is a busy public space with a volleyball game in progress and a TV soap playing on an outdoor screen. It's a drama of everyday life, I'm told. A North Korean *EastEnders*.

Midnight in Pyongyang, and I'm back in my room on the twenty-fifth floor after a celebratory meal with all our guides and minders. Glasses were raised and toasts drunk in beer

and whisky and *soju*. That Neil was so genuinely cordial in his thanks said everything about the strength of the relationship that has grown up between us all. My feelings were guarded to start with. I equated the unfamiliar with the threatening.

As the days went by, I realised my preconceptions were distorted. The North Koreans I have encountered are not malevolent automatons. They are locked in a system which demands unbending loyalty, but which in return offers security, and within narrow confines the chance for some to enjoy life and to excel. Those we have met, and those we saw going about their daily lives, were not broken and bowed, but proud of their country and pleased that we were so interested in how they lived.

For our part, we worked very hard every day, grasping every opportunity a rare trip like this offered. I think our hosts appreciated that, hard work being very much a Korean trait, north and south of the border.

Friendships grew, as did their curiosity about how we lived. By the end Mrs Kim, Tall Li, Yung Un, all so formidably stern to start with, relaxed and joked and enjoyed being with us, rather than just watching us. I'd shown So Hyang photos of my family in London and she had talked about herself and her parents quite openly. This morning as I was about to be filmed, I'd asked her to look after my panama hat. I told her that the best way of looking after it was to wear it. Shyly at first she tried it on. After that, she was clearly reluctant to take it off. Out of the corner of my eye I caught her striking a pose, testing the new look in her reflection in the window of the minibus. That was when I knew at least something of me was destined to stay in North Korea.

DAY 15

THURSDAY 10TH MAY

I'M LOOKING OUT FOR THE LAST TIME AT THE GREY, unpainted tower blocks across the road. The same blank exteriors that had spooked me out on that first morning. Beyond them I can see the river, and the Juche monument with its flaming crest standing very tall on the far bank. The strains of 'Where Are You, Dear General?' resonate from their hidden speakers, once so disturbing, now irritatingly familiar.

I've been quite comfortable here. I've appreciated the neatness, tidiness and politeness of those we've met. I've relished the lack of pollution and not for one moment missed the internet, the smartphone or the jarring, screeching, continuously in-your-face advertising of the West.

So why should I feel something's missing? I think it's because I sense that, for all the access we've had here, for all the increasingly warm relations between us and our minders, they've been playing a game with us. We have been indulged, but never fully informed. We have been allowed more sustained access to this cagey country than most broadcasters, but I still feel that we have been subtly manipulated for some greater end. Was the permission we were given to film just another strand in the policy of detente? The inscrutable nature of power in this country makes it impossible to know what they really want from us. It's obvious that the regime needs to make friends, if only to save their tottering economy. The conundrum for the leaders is how to welcome foreigners economically whilst slamming the door politically. We take freedom of expression to be one of our most basic democratic rights.

Here in the Democratic People's Republic it is one of their greatest fears.

The regime doesn't want its people to be spoilt for choice. They want them to be carrying one thought, in unison, at all times. Love of the Leaders. Total obedience. This is the certainty that has sustained the DPRK since its inception.

But even in the short time we've been here quite big things have changed. At breakfast we hear two contrasting news headlines. Mike Pompeo and his team, who were in this same hotel only yesterday, are flying back home today, taking their freed hostages with them. A glimmer of peace, a hint of conciliation to be followed by an unprecedented summit between American and North Korean leaders. We also learnt this morning that the American President has repudiated the Iran nuclear deal. Trump, it seems, is much more comfortable

dealing with a hereditary dictatorship in Korea than with a theocracy in the Middle East. Only months after calling him a mentally deranged dotard, Kim Jong Un has responded with enthusiasm to the American President's approaches. This is breathtakingly spontaneous diplomacy and who knows where it will lead? Kim sees valuable opportunities for wider international recognition. He must also calculate carefully where this might lead his country. With recognition will come thoughts and ideas that could undermine the very existence of his regime.

Into our minibus for the last time and out to the airport. One final image to take home with me: a chorus line of military mothers waving flags, beating drums and line dancing as the rush-hour crowds come and go in the metro station behind them.

And as we settle into our seats in a sparkling clean and modern Air Koryo Tupolev jet, the screens above our heads flash on, filled with all-singing, all-dancing, if rather younger, ladies. They seem to have no trouble expressing emotion. It pours out of them. The sheer joy of being born a part of the Democratic People's Republic of Korea.

We roll down the runway, lift into the skies and soon Pyongyang is disappearing below us. Whatever qualifications we might have, the trip has been an eye-opener, a chance to look behind the headlines and see this secretive country as few other Westerners ever will. As Pyongyang recedes into the distance, we turn and exchange smiles. Of relief, but also of regret. One thing we all agreed on at our farewell meal last night is that none of us would mind coming back.

THE RECCE

MARCH 2018

MANY FILMING TRIPS ARE PRECEDED BY WHAT IS generally known as 'the recce', when the director visits the locations and meets many of the people they hope to film. Because North Korea is effectively cut off from the outside world, my recce in March 2018 was the first and only time anyone from the ITN production team would have direct contact with the North Koreans before the start of the shoot in late April. I know travelogues can look as though they are really easy programmes to make but most are planned with military-like precision, so this ten-day trip was, to say the least, essential.

After flying to Beijing, I met up with Nick Bonner from Koryo Tours, who was our vital liaison between London and Pyongyang and would accompany me on the trip. I hope Nick won't mind me saying that he is just a big kid at heart, because his ability to use humour and general silliness to diffuse tensions with the North Koreans on the recce and shoot was a godsend.

After catching the overnight train from Beijing to Pyongyang, we were greeted at the station by our North Korean guides, So Hyang and Hyon Chol, and their boss, a man known only to us as 'Tall Li'. All three work for KITC, the Korea International Tourism Company, and together with Nick have been bringing in small groups of international visitors to North Korea for many years.

In the weeks before the recce, Nick and I had many discussions about the locations we wanted to see and the people we hoped to meet. While I knew the capital city Pyongyang would offer up the iconic imagery of the DPRK, such as the giant statues of the Great Leaders, I also wanted Michael to experience the country as a whole. In particular, I was keen to show some of its natural beauty and when I saw photos of the stunning Mount Kumgang region and the beaches of Wonsan, thought they would be a great way of showing that there is more to North Korea than nuclear weapons and propaganda.

Nick had sent on our 'wish list' to KITC, but on our first morning in Pyongyang it soon became evident that someone had reinterpreted it somewhat. I was expecting to be taken to see the metro system during the morning commute and the giant bronze statues of the Great Leaders, but instead we were driven to a very quiet random street in the centre of the city. The guides kept asking me, 'Neil, Neil, how do you want to film this location?' to which I had to respond that I wasn't sure as I hadn't known we were coming here! I then noticed they were both holding their own Korean-language versions of the schedule and when I asked what we were doing later in the week, it became obvious that theirs and mine were quite different. Not only were there no giant statues on the list, but Mount Kumgang was also nowhere to be seen.

Sensing awkwardness, Nick suggested we sit down for a chat in one of Pyongyang's few coffee shops. We then went through the whole schedule and tried to realign it with what had originally been planned. I am still not entirely sure why things had changed; maybe the guides considered their ideas better than mine (possibly they were right), but it was also obvious that some of our requests involved filming in 'sensitive' areas. Mount Kumgang, for example, is located on the west coast close to the border with South Korea, and the whole area is teeming with military installations. But I kept insisting that it was important we showed people a different side of North Korea, and after much discussion Kumgang was back on the schedule. Several coffees later, the schedule was starting to resemble what we had hoped for.

There were, however, some areas that remained 'no go'. We would not be allowed to visit, let alone film inside, the mausoleum where the embalmed bodies of North Korea's former leaders Kim Il Sung and Kim Jong Il are on display to a constant stream of sobbing citizens, paying their respects. More worryingly, Pyongyang's iconic Mansu Hill Grand Monument, where the two largest bronze statues of the deceased Great Leaders stand, was also off limits.

In the past, tourists have been asked to lay flowers by the statues on the first day of their visit, bowing and paying respect to the fathers of the DPRK. Now, Tall Li told me, it was no longer 'policy' for visitors to pay respects with flowers, on the grounds that such a gesture might send out the idea that tourists are being forced to do something against their will. After days spent trying to persuade the guides of the importance of having the statues in the series, I was eventually allowed to visit the monument, providing I behaved myself. But it took weeks to get approval for Michael to film there and then only on the condition that he did *not* pay his respects with flowers.

As the recce continued, these daily tussles with the guides continued, but the problems were often down to a lack of understanding documentary film-making, rather than political sensitivity. For example, they found it very hard to understand why, on the shoot, we would need to spend at least three hours filming most locations when a normal tourist visit would only take twenty minutes.

One such tussle took place over my request to film at a bar. Drinking is very much part of the culture of North Korea and Nick had mentioned beer bars where locals go in the evening to spend their state-issued beer vouchers. Back in London, Michael and I often discussed how keen we were to capture everyday life and what better place to film this than in a North Korean pub? After some persuasion, Tall Li reluctantly agreed to take us by car to a local bar and that evening we drove down a dark back street, passing a fairly basic-looking building that was teeming with people, inside and out. This glimpse of slightly drunk and rowdy Koreans was so at odds with the stereotypical image of Pyongyang as a 'weird' city populated by repressed citizens that I couldn't wait to go inside. But then the car kept going for another hundred yards and we stopped outside a much smaller and much more glitzy-looking establishment that was totally empty.

I asked Tall Li why we had come here and not the other bar. 'This is much nicer' was his somewhat curt response, but eventually he let me walk down to the first one, to look at it from the street. Inside a neon strip-lit room were hundreds of people crowded around trestle tables, chatting amongst themselves and handing over coupons to people pulling pints at the counter. The place was teeming with life and exactly the sort of thing Michael and I wanted to capture on screen, but looking was all I could do. There was no question of me being allowed to go inside, let alone film there.

This kept happening: we had solitary breakfasts in hotel ballrooms and dinners in empty restaurants owned by KITC. It was always easy to get a table, but meals became the dining equivalent of being sent to Siberia.

I suspected the guides didn't want us to see where 'real' North Koreans ate and drank because they thought they were too squalid for us to show on television. But the busy bars and restaurants I saw while we walked around Pyongyang looked perfectly decent, even if they were a little more basic than the tourist establishments. I began to realise that the guides just couldn't understand why filming everyday life was so important to me; in their view it made much more sense to visit the 'best' places, even if they happened to have no people inside.

After four days of this, my patience wore thin. 'I'm trying to make a series about real life in North Korea,' I said, 'and you won't let me see it. So everyone in Britain will think Pyongyang is some alien city with empty streets and empty restaurants because you won't let us film the places people actually go to!'

The message clearly hit home because the next night they took me to a small Korean barbecue restaurant hidden down a back street, which was bustling with life – and customers. We ended up filming there on the shoot.

I sometimes worry that people who watch the series think that the North Koreans controlled our every move and told us what we would do every day. I won't deny that there were heavy restrictions or that everything we filmed had to be agreed and signed off in advance, but the guides gave in to our demands more often than you might imagine. The bizarrely empty airport that Michael visited in Wonsan was off limits to me on the recce, but after much discussion we were granted permission to film there on the shoot. Using a drone camera to achieve aerial shots of Pyongyang was also dismissed out of hand to begin with, but after I'd explained how good it would make the city look, the authorities eventually relented. While there were tensions, it felt as though the guides were working with Nick and me as one team, to help make the filming go as smoothly as possible.

Many of the challenges we faced were the day-to-day ones you might expect in a poor country such as North Korea. Outside Pyongyang, driving was not an enjoyable experience;

road surfaces were uneven and potholed. I doubt we ever drove faster than twenty or thirty miles an hour, which made even short journeys into three- or four-hour low-level torture sessions. And once we were out in the countryside we found that the electricity supply was, at best, patchy; hotels would regularly be plunged into darkness during dinner or as we were brushing our teeth at night. The etiquette seemed to be just to carry on as though nothing had happened, even if the power cut lasted several minutes. Given that modern film cameras need powerful batteries that have to be charged overnight, we were sufficiently concerned that we ended up taking twice the number of batteries that we needed on the shoot just in case we found ourselves without power for a couple of days. In the event, we experienced barely a single power cut once we were actually filming.

As the recce continued, the guides would ask me for every single detail of how I wanted to film each location. I was also told that I needed to present the boss of KITC with a completed schedule for the two-week shoot by the end of the trip, something that would normally be done back in London, in the intervening period between the recce and shoot. As a result, I spent most of my evenings on the recce holed up in various hotel rooms, writing a very detailed account of what we wanted to film each day, what times we would arrive and leave the various locations, who Michael wanted to meet and, very importantly, what subjects he would be discussing on camera.

When we returned to Pyongyang after being on the road for a few days, I was marched into a hotel conference room where our guides were seated at a formal boardroom table with Tall Li and his boss, 'Mr Mun'. The atmosphere on the recce had become very relaxed and informal, but now it was quite different. Mr Mun read me a typed statement in Korean, basically saying that he would consider the schedule I proposed and that he would let us know in a few weeks if it had been approved. He made it sound as though the chances of the filming happening were about fifty-fifty and I left the meeting full of doubt.

It wasn't until Michael and I had passed through North Korean customs and immigration checks on the shoot almost two months later that I knew we were good to go.

Neil Ferguson
Series Director

1 3 5 7 9 10 8 6 4 2

Hutchinson

20 Vauxhall Bridge Road
London SW1V 2SA

Hutchinson is part of the Penguin Random House group of companies whose addresses can be found at global.penguinrandomhouse.com

Penguin
Random House
UK

North Korea Journal
Copyright © Michael Palin, 2019
The Recce
Copyright © Neil Ferguson, 2019

Photographs are reproduced by kind permission of:
Nick Bonner pp. 109, 139;
Doug Dreger pp. 18, 19, 24, 29, 53, 61, 64, 65, 66, 76, 80, 86, 89, 93, 106, 110, 113, 122, 131, 134, 140, 141, 142, 149;
Neil Ferguson pp. 15, 16, 31, 32, 161; Getty Images pp. 35, 41, 49, 77, 144, 151;
Jaimie Gramston pp. 25, 30, 33, 38, 44, 46, 50, 54, 58, 63, 68, 73, 74, 81, 82, 84, 88, 95, 97, 98, 99, 102, 148, 158, 160; Jake Leland p. 138.
All other photographs from author's collection.

First published by Hutchinson in 2019

www.penguin.co.uk

A CIP catalogue record for this book is available from the British Library

ISBN 978 1 7863 3190 8

Publishing Director:
Nigel Wilcockson

Assistant Editor: Callum Crute

Designer: Tim Barnes,
www.herechickychicky.com

Map: Darren Bennett,
www.dkbcreative.com

Printed and bound in Germany, by Firmengruppe APPL, aprinta druck GmbH

Penguin Random House is committed to a sustainable future for our business, our readers and our planet. This book is made from Forest Stewardship Council® certified paper.

MIX
Paper from responsible sources
FSC
www.fsc.org   FSC™ C004592